The Word and the Spirit

In honour of all those subjects of so many oppressive governments in every part of the world who have, at no little cost, taken up the cause of humanity and human freedom and in whom the Word and the Breath of God are revealed as living, as active and as truly Lords, whether known or unknown.

Y. C.

YVES M. J. CONGAR

The Word and the Spirit

Translated by David Smith

GEOFFREY CHAPMAN

London

HARPER & ROW PUBLISHERS

San Francisco

1817

A Geoffrey Chapman book published by
Cassell Ltd
1 Vincent Square, London SW1P 2PN

Harper & Row, Publishers, Inc.
1700 Montgomery Street
San Francisco, California 94111

First published in French as *La Parole et le Souffle* in the series 'Jésus et Jésus-Christ',
© Desclée, Paris, 1984
English translation first published 1986
English translation © Geoffrey Chapman, a division of Cassell Ltd 1986

ISBN 0 225 66433 X (Geoffrey Chapman)
     0-86683-538-5 (Harper & Row)

British Library Cataloguing in Publication Data
Congar, Yves
  The Word and the Spirit.
  1. Holy Spirit
  I. Title   II. La parole et le souffle. English
  231'.3   BT121.2

Printed and bound in Great Britain by Billing and Sons Limited, Worcester

The front cover picture *The Baptism of Christ* from the Baptistery Doors,
Florence, is reproduced by permission of the Mansell Collection.

Contents

Abbreviations

AAS	Acta Apostolicae Sedis
ABG	Archiv für Begriffsgeschichte
ACan	L'Année canonique
APhC	Annales de philosophie chrétienne
BEThL	Bibliotheca Ephemeridum Theologicarum Lovaniensium
Bib	Biblica
Bibl. Aug.	Bibliothèque augustinienne
Bijdr.	Bijdragen
BSHT	Breslauer Studien zur historischen Theologie
Cath., Cath (M)	Catholica
DBS	Supplément au Dictionnaire de la Bible
DC	Documentation catholique
Div.	Divinitas
DS	H. Denzinger (ed.), rev. A. Schönmetzer, Enchiridion Symbolorum
DSp	Dictionnaire de spiritualité
DThC	Dictionnaire de théologie catholique
DViv	Dieu vivant
EL	Ephemerides Liturgicae
EtB	Etudes bibliques
EThL	Ephemerides Theologicae Lovanienses
Et. Théol. et Rel.	Etudes théologiques et religieuses
FGLP	Forschungen zur Geschichte und Lehre des Protestantismus
FV	Foi et vie
GCS	Die griechischen christlichen Schriftsteller
Greg	Gregorianum
HeyJ	Heythrop Journal
Irén.	Irénikon

Ist.	*Istina*
JB	Jerusalem Bible
JR	*Journal of Religion*
KuD	*Kerygma und Dogma*
LV	*Lumière et vie*
Mansi	J. D. Mansi (ed.), *Sacrorum Conciliorum nova et amplissima Collectio*
MBTh	*Münsterische Beiträge zur Theologie*
NJB	New Jerusalem Bible
NRT	*Nouvelle revue théologique*
NS	new series
NT.S	Supplement to *Novum Testamentum*
Oec.	*Oecumenica*
Orien.	*Orientierung*
PG	J. P. Migne (ed.), *Patrologia Graeca*
PL	J. P. Migne (ed.), *Patrologia Latina*
POC	*Proche Orient chrétien*
RAp	*Revue apologétique*
RB	*Revue biblique*
ReC	*Russie et chrétienté*
RHE	*Revue d'histoire ecclésiastique*
RHLR	*Revue d'histoire et de littérature religieuses*
RHPhR	*Revue d'histoire et de philosophie religieuses*
RITh	*Revue internationale de théologie*
RMM	*Revue de métaphysique et de morale*
RSPhTh	*Revue des sciences philosophiques et théologiques*
RSR	*Recherches de science religieuse*
RSV	Revised Standard Version
RThL	*Revue théologique de Louvain*
RThom	*Revue thomiste*
SacDot	*Sacra Doctrina*
SC	*Sources chrétiennes*
Schol.	*Scholastik*
ST	*Summa Theologiae*
TDNT	G. Kittel and G. Friedrich (eds), *Theological Dictionary of the New Testament* [Eng. trans. of *ThWNT*]
ThH	*Théologie historique*
ThQS	*Theologische Quartalschrift*
ThSt	*Theological Studies*
ThWNT	G. Kittel and G. Friedrich (eds), *Theologische Wörterbuch zum Neuen Testament*
VC	*Verbum caro*

Preface to the French Edition

Joseph Doré

Neither Yves Congar nor, therefore, his book needs any recommendation. All I wish to do here is to indicate the potential contribution of the present work to the series 'Jésus et Jésus-Christ' for which this eminent Dominican theologian kindly agreed to write it.

(1) Jesus Christ is the centre of the Christian faith, but he is not the whole of that faith. To put this differently, in Thomas Aquinas' terms which the author himself cites and explains later: though Jesus Christ is the Head of that Body which is the Church, he is not its heart. According to Thomas, whose thinking in this regard is liberal in comparison with, say, Bonaventure's, that is rather the function of the Holy Spirit.

It cannot be denied that what is at stake in Christian faith is God himself and the way in which he acts to save the human race. Though Jesus Christ is indeed the voice and the way by which we may truly know God and his saving action, we run the risk of losing sight of them both if we concentrate exclusively on Jesus. According to strict Christian teaching, it is incorrect to assert that God reveals himself and saves people only through, with and in Christ. The God of the Bible makes himself known and acts only in the union of his *word* and his *breath*, his (incarnate) *Word* and his (communicated) *Spirit*. Irenaeus used of both the admirable phrase 'the two hands of the Father'. The present work aims to show that, and how, these two hands work together. The theological risks and dangers of 'Christomonism' are detected and rejected in favour of a 'pneumatological Christology'. Similarly, any 'autonomism' of the Spirit is repudiated in favour of a 'Christological pneumatology'.

(2) I shall allow the reader to discover at his own pace how Christology as such is enriched by this treatment. Here I shall merely draw attention to the breadth of the theological territory covered, extending as it does beyond the doctrine of Jesus Christ, but still essentially linked to it.

On the one hand, the immanence of God is touched on, for in such a context the implication of the *Filioque* clause has to be taken into account. On the

x PREFACE TO THE FRENCH EDITION

other hand, we are involved with absolutely fundamental contemporary
ecclesiological problems, for it is a question of the relationship between
charisms and the institution (or institutions) and of the connection between
'synodality' and 'cephality'.

The ecumenical relevance of the discussion of all these questions is obvious,
with regard to both the Orthodox Church and the churches of the
Reformation. Here, of course, the author respects a dimension of theology
which, as he says, is 'so close to his heart that it would be astonishing if he
were to forget it'. Whether taking us back to his 'youthful articles' (published
as long ago as 1935!), which he rightly finds 'still worth reading' (see the end
of Chapter 7, p. 117) recalling the beginning (in 1937) of the distinguished
series 'Unam Sanctam' (pp. 115 and 121 note 44), suggesting a *retractatio* in
respect of a position adopted previously (in 1953: see Chapter 5, section
entitled 'Institution and Charism', pp. 58–62; also p. 74 note 37, referring, on
this particular point, to his work often cited here: *I Believe in the Holy Spirit*),
or relying on his now classical *Vraie et fausse réforme dans l'Eglise* (1950) and
Lay People in the Church (Fr. 1953; ET 1957), variously and consistently in
this book Yves Congar ploughs that ecumenical furrow which no one else has
followed for and among us in precisely the same way. It is a performance that
compels our admiration and gratitude.

(3) The reader will certainly allow me to conclude this prefatory note in
the personal vein which the first lines of the author's Introduction seem not
only to permit but to call for. In those lines Fr Congar recalls my visit to him
to commission this book and mentions both his friendly willingness to write
what I asked for and the difficulties which, because of his health, he
experienced when trying to do so. He will forgive me not only for thanking
him once again publicly, but for passing on to his readers the testimony which
in fact I received from him. The way in which, despite the 'times when it was
physically impossible to write' and the periods of exhaustion, he succeeded in
producing this book was and remains for me the vital evidence in a
theologian's life of a fundamental truth. To those whose *words* are wholly
dedicated to the service of his Word made flesh, the God of Jesus Christ grants
in the hour of our trial the grace once again to draw *breath* in his Spirit.

The publishers of the English edition wish to thank the translator, David
Smith, who also translated Yves Congar's trilogy *I Believe in the Holy Spirit*
(Geoffrey Chapman/The Seabury Press, 1983). They are also grateful for
valuable advice and suggestions from Fr Nicholas Tranter, who read the
translation in typescript.

Most biblical quotations are from the Revised Standard Version, copyright
© 1946, 1952, 1957, 1971, 1973 by Division of Christian Education of the
National Council of the Churches of Christ in the United States of America.

Introduction

If I were to draw but one conclusion from the whole of my work on the Holy Spirit, I would express it in these words: no Christology without pneumatology and no pneumatology without Christology. Now my friendship with Joseph Doré has given me an opportunity to offer a more thorough account of my thoughts on this subject and to do it in the excellent series of which he is the editor. It was a fortunate request which I was very pleased to accept. I am afraid, however, that I expected too much of my capabilities. My health problems have become much worse and daily demands have imposed various and often urgent tasks on me. I have often had to interrupt my work and there have been times when it was physically impossible to write. The work that I now put forward is not the one I really wanted to produce. Old horses may die in harness, but towards the end of their lives they do not draw the cart so well.

If we are to believe Heribert Mühlen, Catholics at one time relied on a pre-Trinitarian notion of God, a pre-Trinitarian monotheism in fact. For about fifteen years now, theologians have been mainly interested in Christology. I could cite a dozen or so recent works on Christology, even apart from those in Joseph Doré's series. The great, profoundly Pauline spirituality of Dom Columba Marmion (3 vols, 1918-22) was even then wholly centred on Christ. Some scholars have even been critical of Catholic practice for a Christocentrism exercised at the expense of theocentrism (see, for example, Jean Milet, *God or Christ?* [London, 1981]) or have gone so far as to talk of 'Jesuanism' (see André Manaranche). In 1948, Otto A. Dilschneider put forward an outline of dogmatic theology that was entirely Christological: *Gegenwart Christi (Christi praesens). Grundriss einer Dogmatik* (Gütersloh, 2 vols). According to Dilschneider, dogmatic theologians ought to work out what he called a 'morphological Christology', that is, a view of Christ in the forms in which he reveals the mystery of salvation. In the form of God, he would therefore be the creative Christ. Christ in his cosmic role would refer to the first article of the creed, in his bodily and kenotic form to the second article, and in the form of the Spirit, because 'the Spirit is the form of the presence (*Dasein*) of the pneumatic Christ', he would refer to the third article. The Church and the sacraments would be the form taken by grace. In this way, Dilschneider advocated a Christologization of the creed.

The Christological emphasis of Karl Barth's *Church Dogmatics* is well known. Nevertheless, his view was Trinitarian. Part 10 dealt with God the eternal Father — creation; Part 11 with God the Son — reconciliation; and Part 12 with God the Holy Spirit, the Redeemer. This is fully in accordance with a dogmatic tradition modelled on Calvin which finds expression today, for example, in the work of Ebeling, Thielicke and Moltmann. Towards the end of his life, Barth said that he would like to present the theology of the creed in the light of the Holy Spirit. He did not achieve this desire, but Thomas Freyer says that we can obtain some idea of what he would have produced if we look at his theology of *Geisttaufe* or 'baptism in the Spirit'.[1] That would give us a pneumatization of the creed, if such an unattractive word is acceptable in this context.

In our own Church, in France at least, the First World War was followed by a renewal of spirituality which from its beginnings and throughout its development until the last few years, displayed a Trinitarian tendency in faith.[2] A number of factors helped this tendency: the logic of reality itself, the patristic renewal, a desire for solid theological foundations, and the ecumenical dialogue, in particular with our Orthodox brethren. This led to the Second Vatican Council, which worked with a Trinitarian concept of God.

A notable renewal of pneumatology was grafted on to that tendency. Once again, this was produced by the forces of reality and life, ecumenism and the Council, and finally the breath of the so-called charismatic movement. On several occasions in the last few years I have published, in the *Revue des Sciences philosophiques et théologiques*, a bulletin on pneumatology and sections of bulletins on Trinitarian theology, to which, if I may, I would refer the reader.

What is at issue is the mystery of the uncreated one who is 'Light beyond all light'. How should we speak of this? *Silentium tibi laus*, 'Silence is thy praise'. All we can do is worship. We poor theologians, however, have to speak and to speak of God!

'For what person knows a man's thoughts except the spirit of the man which is in him? So also no one comprehends the thoughts of God except the Spirit of God' (1 Cor 2:11). Our concepts are inescapably finite. We cannot have any concept of God because all our concepts are created. As soon as we state something, we have to deny it. To each of her propositions about God, St Catherine of Genoa added: 'I blaspheme!'

Nevertheless, it is possible to speak of God. If that were not the case, how could God himself have spoken a human language and through human lips and writing? That justifies the possibility of a theo-logy on the basis of analogy. The fact that we can use analogy only from the basis of human discourse about God — the 'analogy of faith' — in no way reduces its value.

Among our concepts or terms, there are some which designate a reality which as such admits of no imperfection. These include such concepts as goodness, understanding, power (omnipotence), justice, being, substance, person, action, life and so on. Admittedly, the way in which we realize these things is inevitably marked by imperfection and should be denied when applied to God. Similarly, we cannot know the way in which these perfections exist in God. How, for instance, are justice and mercy really identical in him? But we can still say something — for example, that God is truth and light and that he is love. Both these things are said by St John. That surely justifies Thomas Aquinas when, trying intellectually to interpret the revealed mystery of the Trinity, he saw the Word, the Son, proceeding by way or by mode of understanding and the Breath, the Spirit, proceeding by way or by mode of will.[3]

Péguy maintained that there was not a single abstract word in the whole of the Bible. Many things to do with God and the Church have been communicated to us in images and accounts of actions. Revelation speaks to us of the Spirit in terms of images: breath, wind and living water, fire and tongues of fire, the finger of God, the dove, anointing, chrism and cloud. And why are we told that God is a rock — and a rock which we ask not to be deaf (Ps 28:1)? But God is also a lion, a spouse and many other things as well. Why is Christ not only the corner-stone, but also a lamb, a lion and so on? Why did he speak to us about the kingdom in parables: 'the kingdom of God is like . . . '? These are images, symbols and metaphors. But what are the epistemological conditions under which they function and why?

Thomas Aquinas' comment is the most illuminating.[4] He often adds the words *similitudo* and *proprie-improprie* to the term *metaphorice*. A metaphor does not define reality in itself and that is why several metaphors may be applied to the same reality. I have just given some examples of this. The same metaphor can, however, also be applied to different realities. A metaphor directly expresses a likeness of effect or action and the corresponding property. God presents himself to us as being as solid as a rock. Christ in his Passion behaved like an unresisting lamb and he is the very antitype of the paschal lamb. To be sure, God is like a rock as far as we are concerned. What we experience as a rock here below when looking for assurance and safety, God is in his fashion. Thomas therefore speaks of a *similitudo proportionalis*.

The content of Revelation determined the fact that it was offered to such an extent in images (and narratives). It is not intended to inform us about what

God is in the same way as we are informed, for example, about the chemical composition of the body, but it is intended to point to our true religious relationship with God. Revelation is made for the sake of our salvation: *propter nos homines et propter nostram salutem.* In order to say what we ought to be for God, it says what God does and is for us. God is not a mineral, but for us he will be like a rock on which we can rely and support ourselves. 'To believe' in Hebrew is 'to support oneself on'. Correlatively, that determines our attitude. It is clear that we shall reach the eternal Trinity only by way of the economic Trinity. The theologian has to follow this way and follow it in faith, trying to interpret and construe the mystery by using concepts. That at least is the tradition of the great scholastic theologians. But it is possible to do theology in a different way, as, for example, St Bernard did. At the risk of remaining imprecise in certain respects, Luther wanted to keep the terminology of the Word of God, while rejecting metaphysics and scholasticism.[5] The many paradoxical and dialectical expressions which he used also presumably correspond to the feeling which he experienced of non-homogeneity between the natural or rational order and the order of redemption.

A symbol is the place where and the means by which we can apprehend realities which the concept fragments in its attempt to reproduce them exactly. It is also apt to indicate the transcendence of revealed spiritual realities. One may take a more rational expression as an adequate statement. Images do not allow such an illusion. Thomas Aquinas comes close to supposing that in this respect the coarsest are the most fitting.[6] Perhaps I should say: the more material, but they can also be suggestive and beautiful. Art and poetry lend themselves to this aspect of showing but not defining and of communicating but not claiming to elucidate. A sculptor friend once sent me one of his works. My response was intellectual. He wrote back:

> Odd works of art which are
> image more than certainty,
>   Luckily!
> — but who does the image reflect?
> at what level of Being is
> what one sees perceived,
> even the person one loves.
>
> The eye is a strait gate
> where the beam of the image
> received diminishes to a non-existent
> point, only to extend —
> reconstituted in-sight.

The insight of words has a
definition, a finish.
which natural things
do not have: they live.

We must be clear about the function of concepts in theology and about dogmatic formulae. Thomas, like Albert the Great or Bonaventure, used this definition of the article of faith: *Perceptio divinae veritatis tendens in ipsam*, 'a glimpse of divine Truth tending towards that truth'.[7] We possess no adequate concept of God and apply created concepts to him which allow us to tend towards his truth, without being able to grasp it conceptually. The most important word in Thomas' text is *in*, a word that is also found in the creed: *Credo in Deum... et in Jesum Christum*, 'I believe *in* God... and *in* Jesus Christ'. We do not, it should be noted, say: 'I believe that Jesus Christ is his only Son', but make use of a statement which says exactly what or who is in question, to express a movement or thrust of faith by which we are taken up. Augustine wrote his famous commentaries on *credere in Deum*, 'believing *in* God'.

I do not underestimate the efforts made by theologians. After all, I have devoted my whole life to theology! But I still consider the highest mode of theology to be doxology. It has been shown to be full of dogmatic content. But it is content to refer, in praise and adoration, to the Reality who is 'light beyond all light'. It anticipates the eschatological communion in which there will be only praise. 'When we have come to you, these words that we multiply without coming to you will cease.'[8]

Can these points help to throw some light on the delicate conclusion that I reached after examining the question which is still unresolved between the Catholic Church — and indeed the other 'Western' churches — and the Orthodox Church regarding the procession of the Holy Spirit?[9] I think that the two sister churches live by the same faith, that indeed it is the same Church historically, culturally and canonically divided into two different parts. But they interpreted the mystery of the Trinity differently, on the basis of different understandings and categories, when confronted with errors and problems that were not exactly alike. I shall return to this question later.

The point is that in faith the most important matter is *tendere*, the orientation or thrust towards what it has in view. To be sure, there is no *fides qua*, no opening or thrust of the subject, without *fides quae*, without, that is, a precise content, but this revealed content which is believed and professed in the Church is open to several interpretations. There have been several approaches to the mystery of the Trinity and others are doubtless still possible: Raymond Panikkar and Henry le Saux, for example, have looked for them within the conspectus of Hindu tradition. The Christology and the

Trinitarian theology of many of the ante-Nicene Fathers was imprecise, but
they gave their lives for the faith, the same faith that we share with them. 'The
originality of revealed truth which lies in its not being a body of doctrine, a
reified "truth" but a dynamic truth, a truth that happens, a practical truth in St
John's sense.'[10] Rather than in theological formulae, this truth is best
expressed in living experience with regard to God and human beings and in
doxology.

Although I am a grateful and faithful follower of Thomas Aquinas, I have
had occasion gradually to extend my vision.[11] Two things have led me in that
direction: ecumenism and the study of history, to which should also be added
an attention (limited, but quite real) to the quests and the writing of today.
Ecumenism and history acquaint us with other interpretations which also
have their own reasons and their own truth. The scholastics were too
encapsulated in their own certainties and in a Church which was closed to any
doubts about itself. Surely our boundaries have become more diffuse! Are we,
living as we do in an inexorably secularized and pluriform world, faced with
only the one way of keeping to the faith and of confessing that apostolic faith,
when there have been and still are so many theological versions of it? I distrust
my own weakness, which I know so well. I rely on my Church, but I would
not want to reduce it either to the level of one of its expressions, even that of
Rome, or to one of its historical aspects, whether that of the Fathers or that of
the scholastics, knowing it to be the living communion of all those who
confess the same apostolic faith.

★ ★ ★

The overall theme of this work is straightforward, but its analysis and its
division into chapters were not essential. I myself was uncertain about the
exact order in some cases — where I should, for example, place the chapter on
the part played by pneumatology in Christology. Nevertheless, the sequence
of chapters seemed to be demanded by the questions which arose. I have kept
to a theological level, but I am sure that in this way I have touched on some
very real problems and needs of the Christian world today, above all those of
the so-called charismatic renewal. For that movement and above all for that
movement — but it is well aware of this — the vigour of a lived pneumatology
is to be found in Christology. There is only one body which the Spirit builds
up and quickens and that is the body of Christ.

24 June 1983   Yves Congar

Notes

1 T. Freyer, *Pneumatologie als Strukturprinzip der Dogmatik. Überlegungen an die Lehre der 'Geisttaufe' bei Karl Barth* (Paderborn, 1982).

2 I append an obviously incomplete list of titles, mostly French: Elizabeth of the Trinity, *Souvenirs* (1909, with several subsequent editions; sel. trans. in *Spiritual Writings*, London, 1962); V. Bernadot, *From Holy Communion to the Blessed Trinity* (London and Edinburgh, 1926); H.-M. Féret, *La Sainte Trinité, Dieu du Chrétien* (*Et. Théol. et Rel.* 448; 1938); J. Viollet, *La Sainte Trinité et notre vie quotidienne* (1938); F. Klein, *The Doctrine of the Trinity* (New York, 1940); R. M. Grant, *The Early Christian Doctrine of God* (Charlottesville, Virginia, 1962); G. P. Widmer, *Gloire au Père et au Fils et au Saint-Esprit* (Neuchâtel and Paris, 1963); H. Barré, *'Trinité que j'adore'. Perspectives théologiques* (1965); G. Lafont, *Peut-on connaître Dieu en Jésus-Christ?* (1969); H. Bourgeois, *Mais il y a le Dieu de Jésus-Christ* (1970); J. C. Barreau, *Qui est Dieu?* (1971); A. Manaranche, *Dieu vivant et vrai* (1972); P. Aubin, *Dieu: Père, Fils, Esprit. Pourquoi les chrétiens parlent de 'Trinité'* (1975); C. Duquoc, *Dieu différent* (1977); H. de Lubac, *Christian Faith: The Structure of the Apostles' Creed* (London, 1986; Fr. orig. 1970).

3 If we remained in the rational order, we could only state the essential perfections in this way. But revelation speaks to us of hypostases (without using the word) and, in God, the essence exists only in a hypostatized form.

4 I have read T. H. Herwi Rikhof, *The Concept of Church. A Methodological Inquiry into the Use of Metaphors in Ecclesiology* (London, 1981). For Thomas, see pp. 167ff. See also Study 8 of Paul Ricoeur, *The Rule of Metaphor* (Toronto and London, 1978). He speaks of the analogy (of attribution) in Thomas Aquinas, on the basis of its origin in Aristotle. Metaphor is something else, but (pp. 276ff.) it is close to the analogy of proportion: 'Metaphor indeed is based upon "similarity of proportion"; its structure is the same in poetic and in biblical discourse . . . "God manifests strength in His works, as a lion in his" '.

5 In a marginal gloss of 1509 on the *Sentences*, Luther writes: *Non est itaque determinatio phisica vel logica, sed theologica. Sicut quasi diceretur: quid est Christus? Respondent logicus: est persona, etc., theologus autem: est petra, lapis angularis, etc.,* 'Thus it is not a physical or logical, but a theological conclusion. As if one were to say: What is Christ? The logical answer is: He is a person and so on, but the theologian would say: He is a rock, a corner-stone and so on': *WA* 9, 91. See also my *Martin Luther. Sa foi, sa réforme* (Paris, 1983).

6 Thomas Aquinas, *ST* Ia, q. 1, a. 9, ad 3.

7 Thomas Aquinas, *In III Sent.* d. 25, q. 1, a. 1, qª 1, obj. 4. See also *ST* IIa IIae, q. 1, a. 6.

8 Augustine in the final prayer of his *De Trin.* XV, 28, 51 (*Bibl. Aug.* II, p. 567).

9 Yves Congar, *I Believe in the Holy Spirit* III: *The River of Life Flows in the East and in the West* (London, 1983); idem, *Diversity and Communion* (London, 1984), especially pp. 98-104.

10 Claude Geffré, *Initiation à la pratique de la théologie* I (Paris, 1982), p. 124. See also p. 131: the dialectic of lived and professed faith.

11   The great scholastics, our masters, were more unwaveringly attached to their
      categories and formulae. Nevertheless, they asked whether it was possible to
      think and speak differently in the treatise on the Holy Trinity with regard to
      'notions', that is, properties by means of which the distinction between the
      Persons is known to us and can be expressed. See also Thomas Aquinas, *ST* Ia, q.
      32, a. 4 and *In I Sent.* d. 33, q. 1, a. 5; Bonaventure, *In I Sent.* d. 27, art. 1
      (Quaracchi ed., p. 478). They distinguished the truths that belong directly to
      faith, *sicut ea quae nobis sunt principaliter revelata, ut Deum esse trinum et unum,*
      'according to what is principally revealed to us, that God is three and one', and
      those that belong indirectly to faith, in the sense that a denial at this point would
      lead to a conclusion contrary to faith. 'On the subject of notions, some
      theologians have entertained opinions contrary to received doctrine, but without
      risk of heresy, for they did not mean to uphold anything at variance with faith. If,
      however, anyone should entertain a false opinion of the notions, knowing or
      thinking that consequences against faith would follow, he would lapse into
      heresy' (Thomas).

1

God is Word
God became a Human Word

The history of the Word began in Israel with the prophets. Later on its lessons were applied to the event of the giving of the Law linked with the covenant, then to a vision of the origins of the world and its peoples. My reflection in this chapter will be thematic rather than historico-critical. Historically, the link between the Spirit and the Word begins with Isaiah and Ezekiel.

The word is an act by which a person makes known his or her thoughts and feelings to another by signs. It is therefore the act of one person addressing another. Animals have a language which is very effective, but they do not have the word. The creation of images, another form of expression, is also peculiar to man. Images too enable a personal and creative subject to communicate with other persons. An 'I' enters into a relationship with a 'thou'. The word is therefore both distance and a bond. It joins two distinct beings who remain different. They are persons. Contemporary thought emphazises the personal and the interpersonal, as well as the values of challenging, questioning, confronting and asking for a reply.

For human beings, the word is the main means of satisfying the need they have to express themselves to other humans and even to themselves. Of course, they possess other means of doing that — there is, for example, gesture, which can express threat, anger, tenderness or acceptance. If self-awareness is involved, it begins with feeling, but we still need the inner word to express ourselves to ourselves as well as the enunciated word in order to enter completely into a relationship with someone else.

I say 'need' advisedly, since for us the word means both real riches and a sign of poverty. What should we be without it? By means of the word we communicate, we receive other persons' expressions of their thoughts, feelings and intentions and we communicate our own to them. We are so used to this that we do not find it extraordinary, but if only we stop to think about it, what a mystery it is! For us it is one means of existing outside ourselves — one means, because action is another.

There are words which offer purely objective information, but there are others in which we hand over something or even the whole of ourselves and which expect an equally personal response from the other person. The signifier — the sign or word — depends on the signified. The latter weighs its words and conveys its character to and through them. If it is a question of the word of God, we shall have many signs by which God makes himself manifest and acts outside himself, yet he is the one who acts. What he postulates outside himself has qualitatively various connections with what he himself is. Theology makes a distinction between traces (creation) and image (man). The Bible reveals a divine plan in our regard, one which ends in a communication of God's life by sending his Word in our flesh and his Spirit.

The word is one of the characteristics by which we exist in God's image. Adam names the animals and even names the woman (Gen 2:19, 23). God himself speaks. But in the first place his word does not arise from poverty. It is born of his generosity, both as inner and as external word. It is the means by which God leaves himself, if that is a meaningful expression, and postulates beings outside himself, that is, distinct from himself. In the second place, word and action are identical in God. In us, they are two independent means of relating to others. We can act without speaking, but our word is not effective in itself. God speaks and it is. His word is effective in itself. Word — dābār in Hebrew and logos or rhēma in New Testament Greek — includes action.[1]

'God' is the Father, the Principle without a principle, absolute Origin. We are told that he is love and light. That is how we celebrate him in our hymns. That he should know and love himself is the direct result of his living nature and his generosity. He also expresses himself in a Word and an Image. St Paul and the authors of the Letters to the Colossians and the Hebrews apply to Christ what the Old Testament says of Wisdom[2] and what they say in that regard is completely in accordance with the themes of the Word and the Image. The apostle John calls this Word the Logos and says that the Word was with God and turned towards him. (Pros ton Theon may have both these meanings, but primarily, as I. de la Potterie has shown,[3] it has the dynamic meaning of 'turned towards the Father'.) The Word is with God, not as a friend is with a friend or as a person with another person, but as our thought is present to our mind. It is the expression and image of our mind. We say ourselves to ourselves. The Word is also 'towards' the Father, since, in expressing him, he reflects his own image back to him. Hence there exists in God a Word which is also his Image and his absolute Wisdom.

If God is to express himself outside himself, in a world, it will be on that basis. It was by this Logos–Image–Wisdom that everything was (created).[4] That establishes the possibility that the world itself is a word of God. But, as the mediaeval authors claimed, it is like a book whose meaning only the Book, that is, the Bible, can elucidate. It is obvious that, if God makes himself known and makes himself visible in the world's history, it will also be by means of his Word–Wisdom. We know that he in fact did that in Jesus Christ. Because he is the image of the invisible God, he is the one by whom this God expressed himself freely in creation and redemption, which are linked by the hymn included in Col 1:15-20, which clearly should be reread. 2 Cor 11:4-6 also links the same manifestation of (the glory of) God in creation, in the face of Christ and his Gospel and in our hearts. In this economy of salvation, the wisdom of God is the wisdom of the cross and life will come from death. And just as wisdom is also an image and the two are the Logos, the Son, so too is it in God that the mystery of the cross is rooted. This is a datum which several theologians have tried to consider.[5] It has to be admitted that there are few more difficult themes! But let us remember that the Logos is, in the eternal present of God, conceived *incarnandus, primogenitus in multis fratribus, crucifigendus . . . primogenitus omnis creaturae, glorificandus*, to be incarnate, the firstborn of many brethren, to be crucified . . . the firstborn of all creation, to be glorified.

According to the Bible, the word of God is not an explanatory principle of the rational nature of the world. It follows a voluntary personal decision of God. It makes known and realizes a plan of God concerning human beings. It is effective: 'For the word of the Lord is upright and all his work is done in faithfulness' (Ps 33:4; see also verse 9), 'And he delivered them from their distress. He sent forth his word and healed them' (Ps 107:19-20). The guarantee of the faithful Israelite was therefore his trust in God's word.[6] As for the apostolic word given and received as the word of God, it is effective by virtue of what it proclaims (see 1 Thess 1:5; 2:13). It is a divine force (Rom 1:16; 1 Cor 1:18; see also 2 Cor 6:7; Acts 19:20). It is active (Heb 4:12) and saving (Jas 1:21). The word of reconciliation (2 Cor 5:19) reconciles and the word of salvation (Acts 13:26) saves. The word of grace (Acts 14:3; 20:32) brings grace and the word of life or the living word (Phil 2:16; Heb 4:12; 1 Pet 1:23) communicates life.

This apostolic word is identical with the Gospel.[7] Like the Gospel, its content and agent is Jesus Christ. Its content, in fact, is the plan of God's salvation realized for us in Jesus Christ, the mystery of Christ. In the expression, often encountered in Paul, the 'Gospel of Christ' (or the 'Gospel of our Lord' or the 'Gospel of the Son'), Christ is both the content and the author, the object and the subject.[8] The Gospel is absolutely pure. It has the truth, holiness and power of Christ himself. It is always an act of God. The word is the form in which it is set forth.

Kittel himself wrote that part of the article '*logos*' in his *Theologische Wörterbuch zum Neuen Testament* that concerns the New Testament[9] and in it stressed the fact that the divine and, we might add, divinizing attributes of the word of life are ascribed to an actual historical Christ who was heard, seen and touched by his witnesses. The Logos who was in God and who was God was manifested historically. He was sent and he came. He who is exalted 'on the right hand of God' *is* the one who was born of Mary and who suffered. He is the one 'by whom everything came into existence and by whom we go (to the Father)'.[10] John and Paul attribute to Jesus the Christ the effects already bestowed on the word by the Old Testament, even that of creation. But the Christ, the word of God who came in flesh, is the principle of the new creation. Eschatology was inaugurated by him and by it.

Peter wrote to those who had been pagans: 'Having purified your souls by your obedience to the truth... you have been born anew, not of perishable seed, but of imperishable, through the living and abiding word of God; for "all flesh is like grass and all its glory like the flower of grass. The grass withers and the flower falls, but the word of the Lord abides for ever" [Is 40:6-8]. That word is the good news which was preached to you' (1 Pet 1:22-25). The word received in faith (obedience to the truth) is that seed of God (*sperma Theou*) by which we are born of God: 'Of his own will he (the Father of light) brought us forth by the word of truth' (Jas 1:18). The seed is the word of God (Mk 4:14ff.; Lk 8:12: the word is *sporos*).

The seed-word, then, is received by or in faith. It is not difficult to understand why theologians, notably Thomas Aquinas, should have attributed to faith the effect of *continuatio*, that is, the attachment, joining, continuity and coupling of sacramental signs to what they signify, which is the Passion of Christ, the principle of their effectiveness.[11] Faith touches and causes to be touched. When the crowd was thronging around Jesus, a woman touched the hem of his garment, firmly believing that it would heal her. A crowd pressed in on Jesus, but only one person had really touched him, by her faith.[12] That faith is the faith of each believer, but it is also the faith of the Church, in which the form of the sacraments is like a continuation of the incarnation.

The word is therefore effective in and by the faith that receives it. It is here, theologically, that the Spirit intervenes. My previous studies and this present one should make this clear. Thomas Aquinas, after citing Jn 14:26: 'He will teach you all things' and Jn 14:6: 'I am the way and the truth and the life', wrote: 'The Son gives us his teaching, since he is the Word, but the Holy Spirit makes us able to receive that teaching. He therefore says: "He will teach you all things". Man may try to learn externally, but his labour will be in vain if the Holy Spirit, from within, does not give him understanding'.[13]

This is, of course, the classical theme of the inner master and one that we shall encounter again later on. It has often been Christologized. Karl Barth, on the other hand, in his great Trinitarian and economic theology of the Word of God, provided a dogmatic systematization of this role of the Spirit. The

Holy Spirit, he claimed,[14] is God in us, allowing and enabling us to believe and to receive the Word as the Word of God, to share in God's revelation of himself and to speak of Christ as the Word made flesh. At its own level, this vision is insurpassable and I shall return to it later.

I will conclude this chapter by saying that, when I was preparing my material for this book, I began by going through the whole of the Bible once again in a search for all the texts linking the Spirit with the Word. This preliminary survey seemed to me to be necessary and I offer the results of it here.

Notes

1   See Lk 1:65; 2:15, 19, 51; Acts 5:32; 10:37, where *rhēma* means 'event'. See also O. Procksch, *TDNT* IV, pp. 91-93.

2   B. Botte, 'La Sagesse et les origines de la christologie', *RSPhTh* 21 (1932), 54-67; A. Feuillet, *Le Christ Sagesse de Dieu d'après les épîtres pauliniennes* (Paris, 1966); P. E. Bonnard, *La Sagesse en personne annoncée et venue en Jésus-Christ* (*Lectio divina* 44; Paris, 1966).

3   See I. de la Potterie, *Bib* 43 (1962), 379-383 and the parallel with 1 Jn 1:1-2.

4   Jn 1:3. The French *Traduction oecuménique de la Bible* notes here that the Old Testament already associates the creation of the world with the word of God (Pss 33:6, 9; 147:15-18; Is 40:26; 48:3; Wis 9:1; see also Gen 1:3) or with divine wisdom (Prov 8:27-30; Wis 7:12; 8:4; 9:9). See also Heb 1:3.

5   Jürgen Moltmann, Eberhard Jüngel and Hans Urs von Balthasar, *Theodramatik* (Einsiedeln, 1980). See also S. Breton, *Le Verbe et la Croix* (Paris, 1981): the cross as word and questioning of the *logos*.

6   See Pss 56:4, 10-11; 106:12; 119:42, 65; 130:5.

7   G. Friedrich, '*euaggelizomai, euaggelion*', *TDNT* II, pp. 707-737. See also L.-M. Dewailly, *Jésus-Christ Parole de Dieu* (2nd revised ed., Paris, 1969); R. Asting, *Die Verkündigung des Wortes im Urchristentum dargestellt an den Begriffen 'Wort Gottes', 'Evangelium' und 'Zeugnis'* (Stuttgart, 1939), pp. 300-457.

8   'Gospel of Christ': Rom 15:19; 1 Cor 9:12; 2 Cor 2:12; 9:13; 10:14; Gal 1:7; Phil 1:27; 1 Thess 3:2. 'Gospel of our Lord Jesus': 2 Thess 1:8. 'Gospel of the Son': Rom 1:9. For Christ as object and subject, see R. Asting, *op. cit.*, pp. 355ff.; G. Friedrich, *op. cit.*, p. 731.

9   '*legō, logos*', *TDNT* IV, pp. 100-136.

10 An alternative translation, based on the *Traduction oecuménique de la Bible*, of 1 Cor 8:6 [cf. note in NJB]. See also Col 1:15-20.

11 See Thomas Aquinas, *In III Sent.* d. 13, q. 2, a. 2, sol. 2; *In IV Sent.* d. 1, q. 1, a. 4, qᵃ 3, sol. et ad 3; d. 4, q. 3, a. 2, sol. 1: *In sacramentis praecipue fides operatur, per quam sacramenta quodammodo continuentur suae causae principaliter agenti et etiam ipsi recipienti*, 'In the sacraments, it is mainly faith which takes effect, by means of which the sacraments are to some extent united with their first cause

and also with the recipient'. See also L. Villette, *Foi et sacrements* II: *De S. Thomas à K. Barth* (Paris, 1962), pp. 45-72; J. Gaillard, 'Les sacrements de la foi', *R Thom* (1959), 290-293.

12 Mk 5:25-34; Lk 8:42b-48. See also Augustine, *Sermo* 243, 2 (*PL* 38, 1144).
13 Thomas Aquinas, *Comm. in ev. Ioan.* c. 16, lect. 6.
14 K. Barth, *Church Dogmatics* I.1: *The Doctrine of the Word of God* (Edinburgh, 1975), sect. 12.

2

The Word and the Spirit are linked
Scriptural testimonies

On beginning a study of the relationships between the Word and the Spirit, it is appropriate first to discuss the Father. In Scripture, 'God' is, after all, the Father. The Word is the Word of God, that is, of the Father. The Spirit is the Spirit of God, that is, of the Father. The Father is invisible and dwells in inaccessible light.[1] The Word and the Spirit reveal him and lead to him. Both the Word and the Spirit first issue from his Mouth.

The biblical applications of this anthropomorphic usage do not tell us very much. In the Old Testament, when referring to God, the Mouth is, with hardly more than two exceptions, the organ of the word.[2] In the New Testament, 'mouth' is often used for 'word'. If it is the mouth of God, it is the source of the word (Mt 4:4) and also of the breath that will 'slay the lawless one' (2 Thess 2:8 and Is 11:4). The breath and the word are sometimes replaced by the image of the sword. It is the word that announces a decision (Is 49:2), divides the faithful from the rest (Heb 4:12) and issues from the mouth of the victorious Lord to judge history: 'From his mouth issued a sharp two-edged sword' (Rev 1:16, 19:15). This formidable prophecy is about the vultures and the destruction of Edom: 'Not one of these shall be missing...For the mouth of the Lord has commanded and his Spirit has gathered them' (Is 34:16). In symbolic expressions, one formula does not contradict another, especially if it uses quite different imagery. Later on, we shall encounter Irenaeus' splendid expression about the two hands of God, which has no biblical precedents.

Scripture, however, often links the Word and the Breath together. In the beginning, the Breath of God hovers over a creation that God brings about by speaking—through his Word (Gen 1:2ff.). 'By the word of the Lord the heavens were made and all their host by the breath of his mouth' (Ps 33:6). When it is a question of God's behaviour towards his chosen people, the covenant comes first. The Isaiah of the exile takes up the theme of royal messianism, the first link in the chain and the first type being David (see

Nathan's prophecy, 2 Sam 7), and prophesies: 'And as for me, this is my covenant with them, says the Lord, my Spirit which is upon you, and my words which I have put in your mouth, shall not depart out of your mouth or out of the mouth of your children or out of the mouth of your children's children, says the Lord, from this time forth and for evermore' (Is 59:21).

Spirit and word are clearly joined in a very special way in prophetic events. The extraordinary Balaam 'lifted up his eyes and saw Israel encamping tribe by tribe. And the Spirit of God came upon him and he took up his discourse and said . . . ' (Num 24:2-3). There follow the words now heard every morning on the Israeli radio service. And there are the words attributed to the dying David: 'The Spirit of the Lord speaks by me, his word is upon my tongue' (2 Sam 23:2). Ezekiel, who speaks so beautifully of the Spirit (whereas Jeremiah says nothing of him), writes, in respect of the glory of the Lord: 'And he said to me, "Son of man, stand upon your feet and I will speak with you". And when he spoke to me, the Spirit entered into me and set me upon my feet and I heard him speaking to me . . . ' (Ezek 2:1-2; cf. 3:24).

The Spirit often leads Ezekiel to a particular place so that he may prophesy. 'And the Spirit of the Lord fell upon me and he said to me, "Say . . . " ' (11:5). The most striking example of this is in Ezek 37, where the Spirit of the Lord sets the prophet down in the middle of a valley and makes him prophesy over the dead bones, a marvellous text!

Prophesying involves an action of the Spirit: 'And it shall come to pass afterwards that I will pour out my Spirit on all flesh. Your sons and your daughters shall prophesy'. As is well known, this text (Joel 2:28 [3:1]) is cited by Peter on the day of Pentecost, as foretelling what has been happening then (Acts 2:16-21), just as the Church in prayer was to credit David with words put into his mouth by the Holy Spirit prophesying opposition to the Messiah (Acts 4:25; = Ps 2:1-2).

Wisdom 'came forth from the mouth of the Most High' (Sir 24:3). In the earlier text of Prov 8:22-31, Wisdom is said to have been begotten by God as a first-fruit of his creative activity. In the Jewish Wisdom literature of Alexandria, composed when the Christian era was drawing near, Wisdom appeared to be so related to the Spirit (see especially Wis 1:6-7 and 7:22 – 8:1) that some early Christian authors believed that they were identical,[3] while others seem to have identified the Spirit with the Son of God, that is, the Pneuma with the Logos.[4] Wisdom was therefore also the Son, the Word, or the Spirit. Wisdom was certainly seen as very close to God and as the activity of God in the world and in human beings. But the Wisdom literature contains no explicit statements uniting the Spirit and the Word.

We do find them joined, however, in several places in the gospels and primarily in the synoptics. I shall deal more fully later with Jesus' baptism, clearly a major event and a Trinitarian theophany. Here, however, I would draw attention only to this one aspect. A voice comes from the Father, while the Spirit comes down and rests on Jesus: 'This is my beloved Son, with whom I am well pleased' (Mt 3:16-17; Mk 1:10-11, which has 'Thou art . . .'; Lk 3:22). The Spirit inspires the words, which are, in Luke, words of admiring praise (see also Lk 1:41-42; 10:21). In the synoptics, the Spirit will cause the replies to be made by the faithful who are handed over to their persecutors (see Mt 10:19-20; Mk 13:9-11; Lk 12:11-12). In this text, Luke combines with the promise of the Spirit's help *in statu confessionis* Jesus' teaching about words spoken against the Son of man, which will be forgiven, and words of blasphemy against the Spirit, which will not.[5] The text of Matthew may be cited here: 'The blasphemy against the Spirit will not be forgiven. And whoever says a word against the Son of man will be forgiven, but whoever speaks against the Holy Spirit will not be forgiven, either in this age or in the age to come' (12:31-32; cf. Mk 3:28-29).

John makes a very close connection between the Word and the Spirit. The Word here is someone quite concrete: the Word of life whom his friends have 'heard, seen, looked upon and touched with their hands' (1 Jn 1:1), Jesus who first had himself baptized by John the Baptist. He came from God. He was sent by God. And 'he whom God has sent utters the words of God, for it is not by measure that he gives the Spirit' (Jn 3:34). Here it is the one who is speaking who receives the fullness of the Spirit. But the sentence 'for it is not by measure that he gives the Spirit' can, however, also be translated as: 'for it is the one who utters the words of God who also gives the Spirit'.[6] Whichever hypothesis we adopt, the fullness of what comes from heaven, from 'God', ensures eternal life and that fullness comprises words of God and the Spirit. Both are present and given in Jesus.

This central theme of John's gospel recurs immediately in the episode of the Samaritan woman. The living water of Jn 4:10 symbolizes both the word that reveals and the Spirit.[7] That is the gift sent by the Father which can lead to everlasting life. But it is already present: 'The hour is coming and now is, when the true worshippers will worship the Father in spirit and in truth' (4:23f.). That means worshipping the Father as he ought to be worshipped, that is, in the truth that issues from him and by the energy that is connected with him. The two gifts, by the very fact that they are so closely connected, always refer to the Father from whom they come and to whom they return.

The extent to which the discourse on the Bread of Life resembles that in Jn 4 is well known. There is the same merging together with an earthly reality and the same request: '. . . Give me this water, that I may not thirst' and '. . . Give us this bread always'. Then, at the end of his very profound instruction on the Bread of Life, Jesus makes this statement: 'It is the Spirit that gives life, the flesh is of no avail. The words that I have spoken to you are spirit and life' (Jn 6:63). It is because the Spirit dwells in them that these words are life and communicate life. The Spirit intervenes as a link between words and life, in this way giving the words their full quality as words of God. As Heinrich Schlier has observed, 'the connection (solidarity) between Spirit and word already emerges from the fact that for the Spirit it is a question of *lalein, anaggellein, marturein, didaskein, hupomimneskein* and *elegchein* (Jn 14:26; 16:13-15; 16:8)'.[8]

I shall examine the expression 'Spirit of truth' later, but in the meantime would stress once more that everything comes from God, that is, from the Father. It is also the Father who, as St Paul says, 'has made us competent to be ministers of a new covenant, not in a written code but in the Spirit, for the written code kills, but the Spirit gives life' (2 Cor 3:6). Here we are in the historical life of the Church, to which Jesus promised: '... the Counsellor, the Holy Spirit, whom the Father will send in my name, he will teach you all things and bring to your remembrance all that I have said to you' (Jn 14:26). Starting with the Father, words and the Spirit are always joined.

In fact, the testimonies we have of the apostolic ministry show the Spirit accompanying the word in order to make it effective in respect of obedience to faith. Paul says this in the earliest Christian text we have: 'For our gospel came to you not only in word, but also in power and in the Holy Spirit ... '.[9] He also provides a similar testimony of his ministry at Corinth (1 Cor 2:4-5; cf. 2 Cor 3:3-6) and, more generally, his ministry to the Gentiles (Rom 15:18-19). This has to do with the preacher: the Spirit takes effect in his words, but if those who hear them accept them in faith, they receive the Spirit, who is the object of the promise (see Gal 3:2, 5, 14; 5:5; Eph 1:13; cf. 1 Thess 1:6; 2 Thess 2:13; Heb 6:4-5). The word is the 'sword of the Spirit' (Eph 6:17).

Peter speaks in similar terms of the message that the preachers of the Gospel conveyed to the Gentiles under the influence of the Spirit sent from heaven (1 Pet 1:12). John calls the Spirit the 'witness' who accompanies the annunciation of Jesus the Saviour and the life of the believing community (1 Jn 5:6 ff.; 4:13, both texts that need exegesis).

To pick out the testimonies to the connection between Spirit and word in the Acts of the Apostles is not too difficult a task, because the aim of Acts is to show how the prophetic mission of Christ was extended by the power of the Holy Spirit (baptism and Pentecost) to the Church and through the Church: 'But you shall receive power when the Holy Spirit has come upon you and you shall be my witnesses in Jerusalem and in all Judaea and Samaria and to the end of the earth' (Acts 1:8). Indeed, as soon as the event occurred, 'they were all filled with the Holy Spirit and began to speak in other tongues, as the Spirit gave them utterance' (2:4). One of the earliest and most widely attested properties of the Spirit is that he spoke through the prophets. As soon as he acts, words are spoken. There is no effective word of salvation other than with

the Spirit. When he was arrested, Peter, accompanied by John and filled with
the Holy Spirit, addressed the high priests (4:8). When they were set free, the
community composed a prayer: 'Sovereign Lord, who . . . by the mouth of our
father David, thy servant, didst say by the Holy Spirit . . .'. At the end of this
prayer, 'they were all filled with the Holy Spirit and spoke the word of God
with boldness' (4:31). When the Apostles were rearrested, they declared
before the Council: 'And we are witnesses to these things, and so is the Holy
Spirit whom God has given to those who obey him' (5:32). The rest of the
account shows the effect of the disciples' words, through the power of the
Spirit: Stephen (6:10), Saul, that is, Paul (13:9); or, in the case of other
disciples, it shows us the Spirit coming down on them and at once making
them speak (10:44f.; 19:6).

The book of Revelation (the Apocalypse) provides not only accounts, but
also visions or oracles. Hearing and sight overlap: 'Then I turned to see the
voice that was speaking to me' (Rev 1:12). This voice is the voice of the Son of
man. It dictates to John the seven letters addressed to the seven churches and
contained in Rev 2 and 3, but each letter ends with the words: 'He who has an
ear, let him hear what the Spirit says to the churches', followed by a short but
very rich and beautiful promise of victory or eschatological glory. Further on
(14:13), the Spirit utters the words that confirm the eschatological end of the
life of the faithful. Like Christ in glory and with him, the Spirit is the author
of the words addressed to the Church. Indeed, the seven spirits — who are in
fact the Spirit — are with the glorified Christ (1:4; 4:5; 5:6; cf. 22:6). The
Spirit is also with those who bear witness to Jesus or carry on the witness
borne by Jesus, 'for the testimony of Jesus is the spirit of prophecy' (19:10).[10]
The Spirit is with the Church and in the Church. He inspires its fervent
desire for the full realization of what it has been promised and for the return of
Christ in glory: 'The Spirit and the Bride say, "Come!" ' (22:17).[11]

Scripture, then, from Genesis to Revelation, that is, from the first to the last
verse, bears witness to the intimate connection between the word and the
Spirit!

Notes

1 Mt 11:27; Jn 1:18; 6:46; Col 1:15; 1 Jn 4:12; 1 Tim 6:16.
2 K. Weiss, 'stoma', TDNT VII, p. 695. The two exceptions are Ps 18:8 and Job
   37:2. In the Septuagint, out of 461 instances of stoma, 109 apply to the revelation
   of the mouth of God, the prophets or wisdom (ibid., p. 697 note 47). Wisdom
   'came forth from the mouth of the Most High' (Sir 24:3).
3 See Theophilus of Antioch, Irenaeus and the Clementine Homilies.
4 Towards the middle of the second century, Justin Martyr and Hermas; homily In
   S. Pascha of the pseudo-Hippolytus.

5　Perhaps wrongly, I preferred this Lucan version to those of Matthew and Mark, the context of which is simply the power by which Jesus exorcizes, in my essay 'Le blasphème contre le Saint-Esprit', *L'Expérience de l'Esprit. Mélanges Schillebeeckx* (Paris, 1976), pp. 19-29.

6　This second interpretation is that of M.-J. Lagrange and of F. Porsch, *Pneuma und Wort. Ein exegetischer Beitrag zur Pneumatologie des Johannesevangeliums* (Frankfurt, 1973), pp. 103f. Porsch argues from the syntax and then from the consistency of ideas.

7　Porsch, *op. cit.*, pp. 139-145.

8　H. Schlier, 'Zum Begriff des Geistes nach dem Johannesevangelium', *Besinnung auf das Neue Testament* (2nd ed., Freiburg, 1967), p. 270. Cited by Porsch, *op. cit.*, p. 201.

9　1 Thess 1:5, which is explained in 2:13, while rejecting the word amounts to a rejection of God, who gives his Holy Spirit (1 Thess 4:8).

10　This text is cited by Vatican II with regard to the witness of the faithful in the Dogmatic Constitution on the Church, *Lumen Gentium* 35, 1 and the Decree on the Ministry and Life of Priests, *Presbyterorum Ordinis* 2, 1.

11　Cited by Vatican II in the Dogmatic Constitution on the Church, *Lumen Gentium* 2 and 6, 5.

3

The Word and the Spirit do God's work together

The Word of God has to be received, but it can be received only by a capacity that corresponds to it. Because we are involved here, the possibility of acceptance has to be present in us. Bouillard, criticizing Karl Barth, spoke of a transcendental condition in this context. This is no more than a potentiality offering itself to be made actual. It can only be made actual by means of an act of God which is called in the Letter to the Ephesians 'a spirit of wisdom and of revelation' (1:17)[1] and by the Council of Orange in 529 the 'illumination and inspiration of the Holy Spirit'.[2] We only 'hear' the word in the way which really allows it to be received and understood by virtue of a divine gift. 'He who is of God (or: of the truth) hears the words of God' (Jn 8:47; 10:3ff.; 18:37). This has been an attested fact from the very beginning (cf. Lydia in Acts 16:14) and down to our own times — God opens the human heart to make it attentive and receptive to the word.

That is why the Church prays for the catechumens. This prayer occurs in the liturgy of the great intercession of Good Friday and John Chrysostom has recorded the prayer of the Church of Antioch, which is so similar to that of the Roman Church: 'Let us pray that God most merciful and helpful will answer their prayers, that he will open the ears of their hearts and that he will teach them the word of truth... May he reveal to them the Gospel of his justice and give them a divine spirit...'.[3] The grace of the Holy Spirit intervenes between the stage of the catechumenate and the situation of the baptized person.[4]

The People of God are invited to listen in order to be constituted as the People of God. For the way in which God manifests and communicates himself is in the first place in his word: 'This command I gave them: "Obey my voice and I will be your God and you shall be my people" ' (Jer 7:23; 11:4; cf. Is 55:3). According to Ex 19:5, this had been the basis or the condition of the covenant — one might even say its essence or reality. Faithfulness to the covenant came about and still comes about in a profession of faith: 'Hear, O

Israel: the Lord our God is one Lord' (Deut 6:4; cf. 26:17). In Christian prayer, this becomes at the beginning of every day the *Venite exultemus Domino ... Hodie si vocem eius audieritis* — the 'O that today you would hearken to his voice' of Ps 95:7. 'Hear' (or, of course, 'listen' or 'hearken') and 'obey' are one and the same. The Hebrew uses 'hear' for 'obey'. What is more, the Latin *oboedire* comes from *audire* — obedience is defined as hearing.

That is what faith essentially is. Paul speaks of 'faith' (Rom 1:8; 1 Thess 1:8), 'obedience' (Rom 16:19) and even 'obedience of faith' (Rom 1:5; 16:26). I would add too that even though this is primarily true of the spoken word, it is also true of the written word, for, in a sense which I shall expound later, the Bible is the word of God.

The finality of the word of God decides its quality, as does its origin. If what we have is the word *of God* and if this word is intended to convert us, lead us to God and unite us with him, it is something other than objective information about things and it touches a different level in us from the one where we come to know 'the elements of the world', in Paul's words.[5] We have therefore to distinguish between an external and an inner word. It is in fact a touch, a disposition which is formed and makes itself known in the conscience (which is called the 'heart' in the Bible). It is an inspiration in the sense of obedience to God. It is very like the way in which God brings prayer about in us. Ultimately, though formed within, this word may possibly be like the one which can be heard or read when it comes from outside.[6] Tradition, however, has less to say of such a word and more of the 'inner master' who enables us to understand external words.

This theme is dear to St Augustine. The fact that it comes from Neoplatonism does not make it any less profound or true in Christianity. In a homily, he cites 1 Jn 2:27: 'You have no need that any one should teach you, as his anointing teaches you about everything and is true ... '. For Augustine this is the Holy Spirit. He continues: 'If his anointing teaches you about everything, we labour without cause ... Here there is a great mystery. Your ears are touched by the sound of my words, but the master is within. We may instruct you by the sound of our voice, but, if there is no one teaching you within, then the sound that we make is in vain ... Without, there are masters, aids, lessons, but the flesh of the one who instructs you within is in heaven. And the Saviour himself has said in the Gospel: "Neither be called masters, for you have one master, the Christ" [Mt 23:10] ... '.[7]

This beautiful theme of the inner master is a traditional treasure not only of Catholic spirituality, but also of Catholic theology.[8] St Gregory uses it[9] and so does Thomas Aquinas.[10] The *Imitation of Christ* turns it into a prayer in an atmosphere that is rather mistrustful of intellectualism.[11] The theme was taken up again in the nineteenth century by Gratry in his fervent book *Les Sources*.

In spiritual theology, another theme has been connected with this splendid one of the inner word — that of the spiritual coming of Christ in those who believe each day and throughout time. Hugo Rahner has traced the history of this theme by way of the use Master Eckhart made of his predecessors.[12] At the philosophical-cultural level of ideas about the heart, Clement of Alexandria and Hippolytus both used this theme of the spiritual birth of the Word, as from Mary, in the Church as virgin mother, and in the hearts of believers. Origen took up the same idea and extended it to include the notion of a daily coming and a growth of the Word in human hearts. That passed into the thought of Greek and Latin theologians such as Ambrose and Bernard. The role of the Holy Spirit is, however, expressed relatively infrequently — see, for example, in Hugo Rahner's study various short texts by Origen, Cyril of Alexandria, Maximus the Confessor, John Scotus Eriugena and Richard of Saint-Victor. But I must return to my principal subject.

The action of the Holy Spirit is well attested with regard to the reception of the written and the spoken word. In Rom 15:18-19, for example, Paul praises 'what Christ has wrought through me to win obedience (to faith) from the Gentiles, by word and deed, by the power of signs and wonders, by the power of the Holy Spirit'. And so we have united all the factors of faith in the word: Christ, the apostolic minister and the Spirit. The same testimony is provided by Peter (1 Pet 1:12) and the author of the Letter to the Hebrews (2:3-4). St Gregory comments on the episode reported in Mk 7:33, when Jesus cured a deaf-mute by putting his fingers in his ears and touching his tongue with saliva. The finger is the Holy Spirit (Mt 12:28; cf. Lk 11:20) and the saliva from the Redeemer's mouth is the wisdom found in the divine word.[13] The Spirit is connected with the word. The text of 1 Jn 2:27 on the anointing of the preacher and his hearer has often been applied in this sense. Godfrey of Admont (d. 1165) was therefore able to say: 'This anointing is the invisible grace of the Holy Spirit, which inwardly illuminates our hearts for the knowledge of God and instructs them for preaching. His anointing, John says, teaches us everything. It is most necessary for the preacher and the teacher, but it is equally necessary for the hearer...'.[14]

All preaching should moreover be preceded and accompanied by an invocation of the Spirit, in other words, by an epiclesis. John Chrysostom, that exemplary preacher, writes: 'What use would a homily be if there were no prayer to go with it? The prayer comes first and the word follows, as the apostles say. As for us, let us persevere in prayer and in the ministry of the word' (Acts 6:4).[15] Elsewhere, I have cited some excellent texts in this sense from Bonaventure and a study on the custom, when beginning a sermon, of asking the listeners to pray and have a prayerful attitude.[16] Calvin's statements in this respect are more traditional. He is less assured than Luther of the effectiveness of the word alone, inasmuch as it announces Christ. To be sure, it has divine power, but it is necessary for the Spirit to instruct the hearts of the listeners from within.[17]

Dom de Puniet stresses the immense value of a rite of episcopal consecration, Roman in origin, which is widespread in the East, where there is evidence of it in Syria from the fourth century onwards.[18] Before the laying-on of hands by the consecrating bishop, the book of the Gospels is placed on the head and shoulders of the bishop elect. This gesture has several meanings. The Gospel is Christ and the laying-on of hands that follows makes the gesture of blessing which Christ, when he ascended into heaven, made over the apostles as a sign of the imminent bestowal of the Spirit a present reality. In the ritual of the *Apostolic Constitutions*, the consecrating bishop says a prayer of blessing during the imposition of the book of the Gospels, while the bishop and priests present pray in silence for the descent of the Spirit. Severian of Gabala (*c.* 400) has this comment on this beautiful rite, which expresses an intimate union between Christ and the Spirit, preaching and the Holy Spirit:

> The presence of tongues on their (that is, the apostles') heads is therefore the sign of the ordination. Indeed, as custom demands, down to the present time, since the descent of the Spirit is invisible, the book of the Gospels is placed on the head of the person who is to be ordained arch-priest and when this imposition is made, all that should be seen is a tongue of fire on the head — a tongue because of the preaching of the Gospel and a tongue of fire because of the words: I have come to bring fire on earth.[19]

The *consolamentum* of the Cathari, the baptism of the Holy Spirit, included a rite taken from the traditional ordination ritual, with an imposition both of the hands and of the book (of the Gospels).[20] This was a baptism for the forgiveness of sins and individual salvation, not an ordination to the apostolic ministry.

Let us stay within the Catholic tradition of the ordination of bishops. This translates into splendid symbolic terms what Irenaeus tells us is the meaning of the most authentic tradition: 'The column and support of the Church is the Gospel and the Spirit of life'.[21] Irenaeus celebrates the actions of the Spirit who accompanies Christian preaching and makes it fruitful. He speaks of 'many pagan nations who believe in Christ. They possess the salvation which the Spirit writes in their hearts without paper and ink'.[22]

If it is a question of 'paper and ink', in other words, of Scripture, the problem is to go beyond the material nature of the text in order to reach the level of what the divine author is saying. Who, then, is speaking and what is he saying to us? A principle constantly repeated by the Church Fathers and the theologians and one which is obvious enough in itself is that Scripture has to be read in the same spirit as that in which it was produced.[23] We have, then, to write 'Spirit' with a capital 'S'. There is also Paul's great text on the veil which Moses put over his face and which prevented the Jews from seeing: 'Their minds were hardened, for to this day, when they read the old covenant, that same veil remains unlifted, because only through Christ is it taken away ... When a man turns to the Lord the veil is removed. Now the Lord is the Spirit and where the Spirit of the Lord is, there is freedom. And we all, with unveiled face, beholding the glory of the Lord, are being changed into his likeness from one degree of glory to another, for this comes from the Lord who is the Spirit' (2 Cor 3:14-18).

The meaning of Scripture, Christ and the Spirit cannot be more closely identified than this. Paul speaks of the 'Spirit of the Lord', but he sees them as in the same sphere of existence and function or of action.[24] The glorified Lord and the Spirit do the same work. The unity of the glorified Christ and the Spirit is functional, that is to say, it is an operative unity. The work to be done in believers is common to both of them and the two 'hands' proceeding from the Father do conjointly whatever the Father, who is Love, wishes to do. When Christians speak of this, they do so both in terms of the inner Word or Wisdom and in terms of the Holy Spirit. Paul joins the two together under the name of the Lord, who became a 'life-giving Spirit' (1 Cor 15:45).

In the case of the written testimony of God, the Spirit causes a great depth of meaning with regard to the mystery of Christ to be read in Scripture.[25] The Fathers and the early Christians practised this form of *spiritual* reading. They often went beyond not only the literal meaning of the texts, but also the typological meaning as it relates to Christ. They sometimes, like Origen, engaged in allegory and subtlety, depending on the acuteness of their minds. If the soul moved by love of God and Jesus Christ can draw profit from such explanations, we must recall that the revealed history of salvation has its historical truth, namely that Christ, who is its norm, came in Judaea in the flesh. 'The testimony of the Holy Spirit always sends us back to the historical testimony'.[26]

The Word of God, whether written or preached, seems also to have a sacramental condition or structure. It is meaningful and effective beyond the material nature of the written or spoken words. In the case of the written Word, Scripture is actually there, rather like the Eucharist. There is, in other words, a 'real presence' of the Word. Like the Eucharist too, it calls for a 'spiritual eating' involving the intervention of charity and therefore of the Holy Spirit. The institution calls for the event. In the case of the preached Word, there is a degree of sacramentality, but in such a form that the spiritual event is less certain.[27] It is an occasion rather than a certain cause. The *ubi et quando* of the Reformation can be observed here — where and when God himself really wishes to speak. That depends on a secret 'mission' of the Word and the Spirit in the preacher or the listener or in both of them.

On one occasion, God spoke through Balaam's ass. The reform of Port-Royal was triggered off in 1608 by a sermon whose circumstances Racine describes as follows:

> A Capuchin who had left his convent for reasons of the flesh and would later become an apostate in foreign parts happened to pass through Port-Royal and was asked by the abbess and the nuns to preach in their church. He did so and spoke with such power about the happiness of the religious life and the beauty and holiness of the Rule of St Benedict that the young abbess was profoundly moved and thereupon resolved not only to practise her Rule in all its strictness, but even to use all her strength to make her nuns observe it as rigorously as she.[28]

God worked through this dubious sermon. But the abbess also retained and put into practice the lesson of the religious life. In different terms with their own particular nuances, the New Testament often expresses this obligation to retain or preserve the word so that it may bear fruit (*katechousin*: Lk 8:15; in the major text of 11:28 the word *phulassein* is found). John prefers *tērein*, to keep faithfully.[29] In two instances, both incomparable and spiritually succinct, Luke uses the same verb with a prefix. It is applied to Mary: 'Mary kept all these things (words; the verb *suntērein*), pondering them in her heart' (2:19) and 'His mother kept (*diatērein*) all these things in her heart' (2:51). Something more than a mere act of memory is meant here. What is involved is living faithfulness, not only of a spirit reflecting about what has been seen and heard, but of a conscience which draws on and respects the consequences and finally of a 'heart' meditating on it and penetrating its depths. Life is nourished with the truth that has been received and retained, and the truth perceived is nourished by the experience of life.

This experience is common to most faithful Christians. It is an exchange or a banquet at which our living faithfulness nourishes truth and truth nourishes our living faithfulness. The image comes from St Bernard and was adopted by Tauler, St Catherine of Siena, Luther and others.[30] Christ is the bread and wine of this banquet, at which we are guests only through the Holy Spirit.

There is another image which also has a link with Luther, that of the 'key of knowledge'. Simeon the New Theologian (d. 1022), one of the greatest Christian mystics, had a very profound experience of light and the Holy Spirit. He reduced this experience to a theme. He reproached bad pastors who have the key of knowledge for not using it to enter themselves and for preventing others from entering (Lk 11:52). This is how he expresses it:

What in fact is the key of knowledge other than the grace of the Holy Spirit bestowed by faith which by illumination really produces knowledge and full knowledge? . . . And I shall say it again: The door is the Son — ' "I am", he says, "the door" ' (1 Jn 10, 7-9). The key of the door is the Holy Spirit — 'He . . . said to them, "Receive the Holy Spirit. If you forgive the sins of any, they are forgiven, if you retain the sins of any, they are retained" ' (Jn 20:22-23). The Holy Spirit first opens our spirit (Lk 24:45) and teaches us what concerns the Father and the Son and he again has said this.[31]

This action of the Spirit together with the operation of the Word is also to be apprehended in the Church as such. The Church is the *congregatio fidelium*, the assembly of the faithful. This and other similar formulae can be regarded as the classical definition of the Church, insofar as it is possible to define it at all. This is especially so in the case of Thomas Aquinas.[32] For faith is what brings about in us those divine realities which we hope we shall enjoy one day (Heb 11:1). Faith ensures a form of contact between us and Christ (see above, p. 12). When Paul lists the ministries that make up the Church, he names those of the word that awakens faith and thus obtains salvation (see Rom 10:8b-15; 1 Cor 12:28; Eph 4:11-12). The origin and growth of the Church is in accordance with the reception and progress of the word and of faith.[33] In this sense, we may accept the statement so often found in Luther: the Church as the *creatura verbi*, the creature of the word, made by the word, its existence or substance consisting in the Word of God.[34] The Word acts with its own power to constitute that community of believers, that flock of Christ which is in fact the Church.

That other maxim of Luther's — *solae aures sunt organa christiani hominis*, the ears alone are the authentic sense of the Christian — is in accordance with this. Sight is for the eschatological future.[35] So long as we do not reduce the gifts of grace by means of which God constitutes a Church to the Word alone, we may retain this notion. Augustine says of the apostles: *praedicaverunt verbum veritatis et genuerunt ecclesias*, they preached the word of truth and begot churches.[36]

This genesis of the Church by virtue of the Word — which is the *semen Dei*, the 'seed of God'[37] — is not only the initial act. Unceasingly the Church is called to the obedience of faith to the Word. There exist in the Church two aspects of its relation to Christ and to the Word which are both normative for its faith: a relation of identity and a relation of confrontation.

The Church experiences the first because it is the Body of Christ. Paul speaks of the Church as if it were Christ (1 Cor 12:12; also his account of the vision on the road to Damascus). Augustine refers repeatedly to this: 'Saul, Saul, why do you persecute me?' He also says: 'If they are two in one flesh, why should they not be two in one voice?'.[38] Above all, in his commentaries on the psalms, he stresses the fact that 'it is the Church which speaks in Christ and it is Christ who speaks in the Church'.[39] Here, then, it is especially a question of the word spoken to God, but it is possible to interpret it as implying that the Church bears wholly within itself the word by which it lives.

This can be regarded as the culmination of the tendency whose history I have described, through which the emphasis has passed from the so-called passive Tradition — what is transmitted or handed down — to the so-called active Tradition, which is the means of transmission and is to all intents and purposes the Church's *magisterium*.[40] It has almost led to a replacement of the principle 'the Church believes because it is revealed' by 'it is revealed because the Church believes it' and even 'because the Church's *magisterium* says so'. This has caused some people to say: 'The Church, by divine mandate the interpreter and guardian of the Scriptures, depository of the sacred Tradition which lives in it, is itself the door by which salvation is obtained. *Sub tutela ductuque Spiritus Sancti sibi fons est veritatis* — under the guidance and protection of the Holy Spirit, it is its own source of truth'.[41]

The idea that the Holy Spirit in the Church is the transcendent principle of Tradition is itself traditional. No so long ago I stressed this and reproduced a number of texts illustrating the workings of the Spirit in major actions by which the Church defines its tradition in faith, especially in its councils.[42] The Church's councils in fact provide us with a symbol like the one that we found so striking in the consecration of bishops — the *etimasia*, in which the book of the Gospels is solemnly placed on a throne.[43] At the Second Vatican Council, many of us found this the most intense and moving moment of each assembly. It was a symbol of Christ presiding over the Council, where his Spirit concelebrated with the Fathers in order possibly to 'define'. 'For it has seemed good to the Holy Spirit and to us . . . ', the apostles and the early Christians declared in accordance with the whole Church (Acts 15:28).

When this *etimasia* is depicted, a dove is often shown above the book of the Gospels: Christ sends his Spirit and the two together enlighten the assembly, which represents the Church. This is an illustration of what the New Testament teaches: the Spirit causes Jesus Christ to be known and confessed as the Father's ambassador and as Lord.[44] He does so in history, that is, throughout successive generations and in the conflict of ideas, the interweaving of events and the emergence not only of new methods, problems and errors but also of conspicuous instances of grace and humble faithfulness. For that, Jesus promised and the Lord sent the Paraclete, a name which is difficult to translate, because it includes so many concepts: Advocate, Intercessor, Comforter and Helper.

He was promised to the apostles *eis ton aiōna*, 'for ever' (Jn 14:16), which

may be related to the statement in Mt 28:20: 'I am with you always, *heōs tēs*
sunteleias tou aiōnos, to the close of the age'. It is, then, not a question of the
apostles as individual persons, but of the historical persistence of the Church
that has come from Christ and the Spirit through their ministry.[45] The
activities attributed to the Paraclete for the Church's historical continuation
are astonishingly complete — he will 'teach all things and bring to our
remembrance' all that Christ has said (Jn 14:26). It is not a matter of merely
material memory. The Paraclete, the Holy Spirit, 'teaches' by 'bringing to
our remembrance'. He makes what we remember penetrate to the depths of
our being. Referring to what Luke says of Mary (2:19 and 51), 'who kept all
these things (that she had seen and heard), pondering them in her heart',
Newman shows that she is:

> our pattern of Faith, both in the reception and in the study of Divine
> Truth. She does not think it enough to accept, she dwells upon it; not
> enough to possess, she uses it; not enough to assent, she develops it; not
> enough to submit to Reason, she reasons upon it; not indeed reasoning
> first, and believing afterwards, with Zacharias, yet first believing without
> reasoning, next from love and reverence, reasoning after believing. And
> thus she symbolizes to us, not only the faith of the unlearned, but of the
> doctors of the Church also, who have to investigate, and weigh, and define,
> as well as to profess the Gospel; to draw the line between truth and heresy;
> to anticipate or remedy the various aberrations of wrong reason; to combat
> pride and recklessness with their own arms; and thus to triumph over the
> sophist and the innovator.[46]

That is what the Church has done in the course of time — the Church which
Hugo Rahner has called the 'Mary of world history'. It is the work of its
Tradition, of which the Spirit is the transcendent Subject — the Spirit who
moved Christ and the apostles to utter their words and who still moves the
Church, the structured People of God, to keep and meditate on them. It is
always a matter of what concerns Christ, of what his acts and words mean for
us. It is the same in the case of this second promise concerning the sending of
the Paraclete (Jn 16:12-15): 'I have yet many things to say to you, but you
cannot bear them now. When the Spirit of truth comes, he will guide you into
all the truth (*hodēgēsei humas eis tēn alētheian pasan*), for he will not speak
(*lalēsei*) on his own authority, but whatever he hears he will speak (*hosa
akousei lalēsei*) and he will declare to you (*anaggelei*) the things that are to
come. He will glorify me, for he will take what is mine and declare (*anaggelei*)
it to you. All that the Father has is mine; therefore I said that he will take what
is mine (*ek tou emou lambanei*) and declare (*anaggelei*) it to you'.

The Spirit will speak — he is the Spirit of truth. He will do so by taking or receiving (*lēmpsetai*) from Christ who did not himself speak about himself, but of what he saw and heard of his Father.[47] Guidance in all the truth is guidance (*hodēgēsai*) in the way and the truth which Jesus is: *egō eimi hē hodos kai hē alētheia*, 'I am the way and the truth' (Jn 14:6). The Spirit's role is to communicate, to announce. Above, it was to help to make what our memory makes present penetrate to the depths of our being. This role of the Spirit, however, goes beyond that of memory because he also communicates *ta erchomena*, 'the things that are to come'. He will do so in communicating what he hears by receiving from Christ. That is, from the glorified Christ, who is the same Christ who speaks in the flesh (*eme doxasei, ek tou emou lēmpsetai*). 'The things that are to come' are the future of Christ, what there will be of Christ in historical time. That is why his communication constitutes a glorification of Christ who, in his turn, glorifies the Father. The reference of the Spirit to the Word is complete, but the affirmation of the Father's monarchy is no less complete.

The same thing is expressed in Jn 15:26-27 in terms of bearing witness: 'When the Counsellor (Paraclete) comes, whom I shall send to you from the Father (*para tou Patros*), even the Spirit of truth, who proceeds from the Father (*para tou Patros ekporeuetai*), he will bear witness to me; and you also are witnesses, because you have been with me from the beginning'. Here we have everything regarding the unity of this function of 'witnessing' which comes from the Father, is given by the Spirit, concerns Jesus and continues in the Church through the apostolate. The Spirit proceeds from the Father as the Spirit of truth and the glorified Christ sends him from the Father so that in and through the Church, he may bear witness to Jesus. Through the Spirit–truth the truth brought by Jesus is made present and active in the Church.

John was writing, possibly at Ephesus, when faith and the Church had already spread to some extent. We know from the Acts of the Apostles what had happened: 'And we are witnesses to these things (*rhēmatōn*, words) and so is the Holy Spirit whom God has given to those who obey him', say the apostles (Acts 5:32). John himself is precise about the content of this bearing witness: Christ sent by the Father as Saviour (see 1 Jn 4:13b-14, which corresponds to the text at the [original] end of John's Gospel, 20:31). John, however, also states that this bearing witness of the Spirit–truth initiates what makes the Church, faith in Jesus the Son of God, baptism and the Eucharist (see 1 Jn 5:5-8).[48] Hence the apostle John leads us to the life of the Church and its history, though he also makes statements which have been said to be redolent of individualism, but are in fact more concerned with inner experience.

This problem of agreement between inner personal inspiration and the external and common means of God's revelation of himself was Luther's problem, when he was confronted, from 1522 onwards, by those whom he called *Schwärmer* or 'enthusiasts': Nicholas Storch, Thomas Münzer, Carlstadt and the Anabaptists. Luther was no less convinced than they were of the necessity of the inner action of the Spirit to make us understand the Word of God. In his commentary on the *Magnificat* (1521), for example, he said:

> To understand this holy canticle properly, it should be noted that the Virgin speaks after having had a personal experience in which the Holy Spirit has filled her with light and taught her. For no one can understand God or his Word if he has not been enlightened by the Holy Spirit. The action of the Holy Spirit has to be experienced, sustained and felt and it is in undergoing these experiences that one passes through the school of the Holy Spirit. If one has not gone through it, words remain no more than words. We can know God only through the work that he does in us, through what he makes us suffer and experience.[49]

But Luther also linked the inner working of the Spirit with the hearing of the Word. The Word was for him the means *par excellence* of communicating grace, which awakened faith: *Solum verbum est vehiculum gratiae.*[50] He therefore accused the falsely inspired of appealing to the Spirit independently of the Word. He made the same accusation in the case of the papists, according to whom the Pope made true decisions *in scrinio pectoris sui*, that is, in the chamber of his own judgement, without submitting to the Word. That is what he formulates as follows in the Schmalkaldic Articles, where he expresses his party's position to the Council which Pope Paul III had called at Mantua:

> With regard to these matters which have to do with the external spoken word, the following has to be firmly maintained: that God gives no one his Spirit or grace, unless by or with a previous external word. That is our safeguard against the enthusiasts, in other words, those spirits who delude themselves that they possess the Spirit independently of the word and before it and who accordingly judge, interpret and hear Scripture or the spoken word as they wish. That is what Münzer did and that is what is done today by many people who would like to be judges, distinguishing the spirit from the letter, but who do not know what they say or teach. Papism is also pure enthusiasm, for the Pope pretends 'to hold all rights in the casket of his heart' and that everything that he decides or ordains with his Church is spirit and must be maintained to be just, even if it goes beyond Scripture or the spoken word and even contradicts them... That is why we have the duty and are obliged to maintain that God does not

wish to enter into relations with us men by any means other than his external word and the sacraments. All that is said of the Spirit independently of this word and of the sacraments is the devil.[51]

Calvin was even more systematic in his formulation of a theology of bearing inner witness by the Spirit.[52] He even attributed to this form of bearing witness such a demonstrative effect that it allowed him to decide which were the inspired books and to pick them out from others, just as one 'tells light from darkness, white from black and bitter from sweet'. Luther relied on the criterion, a kind of canon within the canon, of what speaks of Christ and leads towards him. But Calvin encountered the same opponents, the Anabaptists, whom he called the 'fantastics'. In opposition to them, he maintained the sensible position that 'God works in two ways in us, within by his Spirit and without by his word'. He expressed the relation between the two in these terms: 'attach by a common bond', 'instrument of' and 'conjointly with'. He was very fond of the last expression and it is very significant in his writings.

This position of the two greatest Reformers is close to the heart of my own investigation, which is concerned with the links between the Word and the Breath, the Word and the Spirit. To judge from the texts I have just cited, there was, however, a certain danger of individualism. History shows that this was no imaginary danger. What is more, the interwoven history of the ecumenical movement and the renewal of interest in the reality of the 'Church' has led me to look for the bearing witness of the Spirit not only in the believing individual, but also in the believing community of the Church. I would in this connection like to quote Théo Preiss:

> There is much work to be done on the witness which the Holy Spirit bears to the Church. This work is all the more urgent in that we have not yet thrown off our Protestant individualism. If the Spirit gives each individual the assurance that Christian witness is indeed the Word of God and that he is saved in Jesus Christ, this witness and this assurance are given to him and renewed only if he lives in the communion of the Church. A fact which everyone experiences is that the Church does not allow us to see more than a few pages of the Bible simultaneously and that we have to rediscover the others. Theology is therefore the concern of all the members of the body of Christ.[53]

This is a very adequate summary of what is known as Tradition, the dogmatic substance of which is a correct interpretation of Scripture or an exact and profound vision of the work of God to which Scripture bears witness. It is just as much an expression of the Church and its life. Basically, it is the same thing. Did the Second Vatican Council not say that in communicating the

Tradition received from the apostles, the Church 'hands on to each generation *omne quod ipsa est, omne quod credit* — everything that it is itself and everything that it believes'.[54] As R. Marlé, who has specialized in hermeneutical problems, has quite correctly pointed out: 'The Catholic Church lives on the conviction that the gift of the Holy Spirit does not consist in an independent light thrown on the historical manifestation of the meaning of Scripture, and that this historical manifestation is merged with the Church itself. Thus, the discovery of this meaning of Scripture can be no more made apart from the totality of this history in which it is realized, than it can be made apart from the hierarchical institution which assures its authenticity'.[55]

These last few words present us with a difficulty. Admittedly there has been a rediscovery of Tradition and the Church in Protestantism. In my study *Tradition and Traditions*, published in French in 1963 and in English in 1966, I tried to provide a balanced account on the eve of the Faith and Order Conference of the World Council of Churches at Montréal, the culmination of this process.[56] It is very substantial, but we are still confronted with the role of ordained ministers, which remains the most delicate question in the entire ecumenical movement. It is not so much that Protestantism rejects or misunderstands the part played by ministers in what we call the *actus tradendi* or active Tradition. Calvin made positive assertions about this point, but his present-day disciples unfortunately often fail to go as far as this.[57] We have to acknowledge, however, that the radical question asked by the Reformers is still with us: does the Catholic Church not identify itself with its norm, situating it within itself? Consequently, it has had no confrontation, no Lord, no dialogue except with itself. And, since it has attributed all the charism of the Church to the Pope personally, does it not attribute to that same Pope an excessive degree of sovereign normative autonomy? Have we not heard it said: *Sibi ipsi est fons?*

First we have to situate the *magisterium* — and especially the pontifical *magisterium* — within the totality of the People of God, which represents the fullness of spiritual gifts. This is what calls for our respect in the Orthodox theology of *sobornost*, community, which involves a particular anthropology and pneumatology.[58] It has been well enough demonstrated in the case of local or particular churches and special ministries, and is in no way alien to our general theme. What can be detected in it is a relationship between the Spirit, present in every believer and entrusted to the community as such, and the structure that has emerged from the work of the incarnate Word.

We may, however, also see an instance of that relationship in the necessity felt by the so-called *traditum* or passive Tradition and above all by Scripture, the sovereign document bearing witness to God's self-revelation. The problem is a real one. There is no difficulty in principle, since the Catholic Church keeps to this obligation, a rule that was renewed by the Second

Vatican Council.[59] But is the practice wholly satisfactory?[60] Surely there is still a need for the Reformation to disturb us and confront us with searching questions? I would certainly reply affirmatively to this, but I also think that Protestantism for its part should also listen to what the Catholic and the Orthodox Churches have to say. In fact, the three realities — the normative documents, the sense of faith of the People of God and the charism of ordained ministers — have to be seen as a single whole. They complete and in a sense also condition one another. They should function together. Each one, considered by itself and separate from the other two, is no longer what God intended it to be.

The area of the sacraments and the liturgy derives, like that of the living word, from the two hands of God. It is also primarily the word — that is abundantly clear. Augustine even calls the sacrament the *verbum visibile*, a word that becomes visible; this was a formula the sixteenth-century Reformers liked. Karl Rahner developed the idea that the sacraments are the word at its highest level, as applied to the most decisive acts of human life. I consider that the concept 'word' is inadequate here and that the sacramental act adds an original value, that of physical contact that is open to man's senses, the result of contact with Jesus' humanity.[61] It is, of course, a classical doctrine: the sacraments as the result of the incarnation, the sacrament of God's grace. One thirteenth-century author calls the sacraments *reliquiae incarnationis*.

The action of the Holy Spirit is, however, also needed. In their sign-structure, the sacraments exist as things that are offered objectively. They point to a personal use or application: 'I baptize *you*', 'I absolve *you*', 'May the body of our Lord Jesus Christ preserve *your* soul to everlasting life'. The deprecatory formulae of the Eastern rite are no less personal. The sacrament aims at a spiritual effect which, though individualized, is essentially 'communional' in that it unites the individual to the entire Church community as the Body of Christ and to Christ himself. It is the work of the Holy Spirit who, unique and the same, is the principle of holy life in Jesus and in his members. The Spirit, who ensures that the Word of God is heard in words, offers communion with the Passover of Christ in the signs which represent it. Even in the sign-reality formed by the 'eucharisted' bread and wine.

In the Middle Ages, one question, pointless only at first sight, was frequently asked: *Quid sumit mus?* — What is taken or received by a mouse that nibbles a consecrated host? Even Luther, who was a eucharistic realist, would have replied: 'It nibbles the body of Christ', but he would have added at once that it does not practise communion with the truth of Christ the Saviour, since for that faith is necessary. In fact, the Holy Spirit is also needed, as I have tried to show elsewhere.[62] He intervenes in the vital faith and love by which we have communion with what we have received.

If there is a sacrament in which the action of the Spirit has to be acknowledged, it is the sacrament of holy orders. The real continuity of the juridical mission calls for the gift of the Spirit and the Spirit is not a gift communicated merely by the laying-on of hands. He is invoked in the epiclesis in which the whole community shares. The community has already taken part in the awakening and maturing of a vocation and in the choice of an individual or the approval of his selection. Orders, like the Church, have a Trinitarian status. In a highly Christological structure, the Spirit has to give life to everything.

That, finally, is the nature of the entire liturgy. The dogmatic Encyclical Letter of Pius XII, *Mediator Dei*, of 20 November 1947, and the conciliar Constitution *Sacrosanctum Concilium* of 4 December 1963 — which, strange to say, does not cite the Encyclical — provide a very profound definition of the liturgy, calling it a common action of Christ and his Body, the Church: 'Rightly, then, the liturgy is considered as an exercise of the priestly office of Jesus Christ. In the liturgy the sanctification of man is manifested by signs perceptible to the senses and is effected in a way which is proper to each of these signs; in the liturgy full public worship is performed by the Mystical Body of Jesus Christ, that is, by the Head and his members'.[63] This is a very Christological concept. It is both profound and appropriate, but at the same time the operation of the Holy Spirit is not made explicit in it. For it is the Holy Spirit who makes the work of Christ present in the time of the Church and its doxology. He concelebrates with us in order to make Christ's work a reality here and now. It is the Holy Spirit who gives time, which he penetrates and dominates, that special quality which makes it sacramental time, in which the commemoration of the past makes it present, active and effective with the absolute future in view. It is right, then, to complete a Christological vision of the liturgy with the pneumatological understanding found, for example, in Jean Corbon's book *Liturgie de source* (Paris, 1980).

The presence and activity of the Spirit sometimes takes striking forms, the most spectacular of all perhaps occurring at the first Pentecost, when the Breath suddenly produced a sound 'from heaven like the rush of a mighty wind' (Acts 2:2). Usually, however, the Spirit is an inner whispering and even silence. It is the Word that is expression and inspiration. The breath comes from elsewhere — from the Father. And, conjointly with the Word, the Son, it takes us elsewhere — to the Father. The liturgy is a place of 'eternal life'.

Notes

1   See 1 Cor 2:10; 2 Cor 4:3-6; Phil 3:15; Mt 16:17. See also R. Latourelle, *Théologie de la Révélation* (Paris, 1963), pp. 403ff.

2   Council of Orange, can. 7 (*DS* 377); also cited by the First Vatican Council, session III, c. 3 (*DS* 3010). See R. Aubert, *Le problème de l'acte de foi* (Louvain, 1945), pp. 10f.

3   John Chrysostom, *Huit catéchèses baptismales inédites*, intro. A. Wenger (*SC* 50 [1957]), p. 70.

4   See Cyril of Jerusalem, *Procat.* 6 (*PG* 33, 344) and *Cat.* VI, 29 (*PG* 33, 589). See also Augustine, cited in note 7 below.

5   Col 2:8 (not RSV). There is a somewhat different emphasis in Gal 4:3 and 9; Col 2:20.

6   Thomas Aquinas, *De Ver.* q. 18, a. 3: *Est etiam quaedam locutio . . . interior, qua loquitur (Deus) nobis per inspirationem internam. Dicitur autem ipsa interior inspiratio locutio quaedam ad similitudinem exterioris locutionis: sicut enim in exteriori locutione proferimus ad ipsum audientem non ipsam rem quam notificare cupimus, sed signum ipsius rei, scilicet vocem significativam, ita Deus interius inspirando non exhibet essentiam suam ad videndum, sed aliquod suae essentiae signum, quod est aliqua spiritualis similitudo suae sapientiae* ('It is that inner speech by which God speaks to us through inner inspiration. But that same inner inspiration is like external speech. As in external speech, we offer the hearer not the actual thing which we wish to make known, but a sign of that thing, what is clearly a meaningful expression of it. The inner God, while inspiring us, does not therefore offer us his very essence for our inspection, but only, as it were, a sign of that essential nature, which sign is, so to speak, an image of his spiritual wisdom').

7   Augustine, *In Ep. Ioann. ad Parthos* III, 13 (*PL* 35, 2004). He returns to this a little later: IV, 1 (*PL* 35, 2005). Other noteworthy passages are: *In Ioann. ev.* 96, end of 3 (the difference between a catechumen and a baptized person) and the whole of 4 on the Holy Spirit and charity (*PL* 35, 1875 and 1876); 20, 3 (*PL* 35, 1537: *habemus enim intus magistrum Christum* — 'For we have Christ as our master within'); *Ep.* 120, 1, 2 and 3, 14 (*PL* 33, 453 and 459).

8   J. Alfaro has supplied references for the period of the Fathers and the Middle Ages: see *Greg* 44 (1963), 779, 780 note 357.

9   Gregory the Great, *Moralia* V, 28, 50 (*PL* 75, 704-705); XXVII, 41-43 (*PL* 76, 422-424); applied to the anointing by the Spirit, *In Ev. hom.* II, 30, 3 (*PL* 76, 1222).

10 See Thomas Aquinas, *De Ver.* q. 11, a. 11, a. 1, c. end; *ST* q. 117, a. 1, ad 1; *In Ioann.* c. 14, lect. 6.

11 *The Imitation of Christ*, III, c. 2.

12 Hugo Rahner, 'Die Gottesgeburt. Die Lehre der Kirchenväter von der Geburt Christi aus dem Herzen der Kirche und der Gläubigen', *Symbole der Kirche. Die Ekklesiologie der Väter* (Salzburg, 1964), pp. 11-87; the original text dates from 1935.

13 Gregory, *In Ezech.* I, 10, 20 (*PL* 76, 893-894).

14 Godfrey of Admont, *Hom. fest.* VI (*PL* 174, 651Cff.).

15 John Chrysostom, *Homily* 3 on the incomprehensibility of God (*PG* 48, 725-726; *SC* 28 [1970], pp. 219-221).

16 See Yves Congar, *I Believe in the Holy Spirit* III (London and New York, 1983), pp. 109-114.

17   See W. Kreck, 'Parole et Esprit selon Calvin', *RHPhR* 40 (1960), 213-228.
     Calvin combines his idea of predestination with this view by making a distinction
     between the general call through preaching and a special call through the
     illumination of the Spirit, who manifests himself only in believers and the elect.

18   P. de Puniet, *Le Pontifical romain. Histoire et commentaire* II (Paris and Louvain,
     1931), pp. 31ff.; P. Batiffol, 'La liturgie du sacre des évêques dans son évolution
     historique', *RHE* 23 (1927), 733-763; J. Lécuyer, 'Note sur la liturgie du sacre
     des évêques', *EL* 66 (1952), 369-372; *idem*, 'La grace de la consécration
     épiscopale', *RSPhTh* 36 (1952), 389-417; J. H. Crehan, 'The Typology of
     Episcopal Consecration', *ThSt* 21 (1960), 250-255; C. Munier, *Les Statuta
     Ecclesiae Antiquae* (Paris, 1960), pp. 177-181.

19   Severian of Gabala, text preserved in a sequence on Acts (*PG* 125, 533), cited and
     translated by J. Lécuyer, *op. cit.* Also attributed to Severian in the *Opera
     Chrysostomi* (*PG* 56, 404: a sermon on the single origin of the old and the new
     Law) is this other sense of the rite: 'As the high priest was the head of the people,
     he had to have a power over his head — for unlimited personal power is
     intolerable, and so a power which has above it the symbol of its rule is subject to
     law. That is why Scripture has decreed that the high priest should have his head
     covered, so that the head of the people may understand that he has a power above
     (over) him. For this reason too, the Church puts the Gospel of Christ on the
     heads of bishops at their consecration, so that the bishop-elect may understand
     that he has been given the true crown of the Gospel and that, even though he is
     the head (the chief) of everything (of all), he is nevertheless subject to the law of
     the Gospel'.

20   See the *Rituel cathare*, Intro., critical text, Fr. trans. and notes by C. Thouzellier:
     SC 236 (Paris, 1977), text pp. 256-257; history of the Catholic rite, pp. 105-119.

21   Irenaeus, *Adv. Haer.* III, 11, 8 (*PG* 7, 885; *SC* 211, p. 161). The reference is to 1
     Tim 3:15.

22   *Adv. Haer.* III, 4, 2 (*PG* 7, 855C; *SC* 211, p. 47). The quotation is from 2 Cor
     3:3.

23   Texts and references in Yves Congar, *Tradition and Traditions* (London and New
     York, 1966), pp. 91 and note 1, 387 and note 1; see also J. Gribomont, 'Esprit
     Saint', *DSp* IV.2, col. 1270.

24   See *I Believe in the Holy Spirit*, *op. cit.* (note 16), I, pp. 32-33.

25   Paschasius Radbert (d. 865) writes: *Est autem et sacramentum in Scripturis divinis
     ubicumque sacer Spiritus in eisdem interius aliquid efficaciter loquendo operatur*
     ('But there is also a sacrament in the Holy Scriptures wherever the Holy Spirit is
     within them, at work in some way by speaking effectively'): *De corpore et sanguine
     Domini* (*PL* 120, 1275-1276).

26   B. D. Dupuy, *Ecriture et Tradition. Journées oecuméniques de 1968* (Chèvetogne,
     1970), p. 96.

27   See my article 'Valeur sacramentelle de la parole', *VS* 644-645 (May–August
     1981), 179-189. Otto Semmelroth has attempted to define the status of the
     causality of the word in his *Wirkendes Wort* (Frankfurt, 1961). He takes the
     sacraments as his model for the causality of grace, but shows that word and
     sacrament are two inseparable aspects of the one work of grace which God has

38 THE WORD AND THE SPIRIT

entrusted to the Church: 'Even if they take place one after the other, preaching and sacraments are complementary in a unity of total representation, therefore from a place that is different from the unity of causal action' (p. 233); 'The preaching of the word and the distribution of the sacraments seem to me to be two partial but connected stages of the total reality in dialogue form. It is therefore possible to say that the preaching of the word of God possesses all the more effective grace when it is not only more closely but also more visibly connected with the sacrament' (p. 242). Semmelroth relates these two aspects, both as distinct and as intimately connected, to the Incarnation and the redemptive Passion respectively. His approach is, however, entirely Christological and ecclesiological and he hardly mentions the Holy Spirit at all.

28 Jean Racine, *Abrégé de l'histoire de Port-Royal*, ed. A. Gazier (1908), p. 3.

29 Jn 8:51f.; 14:23; 15:20; 17:6; 1 Jn 2:5; Rev 1:3; see also Mt 28:20.

30 Luther's text is as follows: *Nos sumus potus Christo et veritati, et veritas ac Christus e contra potus noster, quia epulamur cum Domino in mutuo convivio pinguissimo ipse nobiscum et nos cum illo, dum invicem incorporamur* ('We are intoxicated with Christ and the truth, and the truth and Christ are conversely our intoxication, for we feast with the Lord at the most sumptuous of banquets, he with us and we with him, and while we feast we are incorporated into one another'): *Dictata super Psalterium* (Ps 68: *WA* 3, 434, pp. 20-22); Tauler, *Predigten* (Vetter edition, no. 60), pp. 292-298, who cites St Bernard, p. 294: cf. *In Cant. sermo* 71, 5 (*PL* 184, 1123). Luther did not know Catherine of Siena, who is in any case less explicit: in giving oneself to Christ, one gives him to drink (*Letter* 22, 8 to Brother Giusto, the Prior of Mount Olivet).

31 Simeon the New Theologian, *Catéchèse* XXXIII, Fr. trans. J. Paramelle (*SC* 113, 255ff.). It may be noted that, in the Roman liturgy for the Octave of Pentecost, the Gospel of Jn 10 was set for Tuesday, when the offertory was *Portas coeli aperuit Dominus* . . . ('The Lord opened the gates of heaven . . . '). For Luther, see his Preface to the *Kirchenpostille* (*WA* 10, 1), p. 16.

32 I hope one day to be able to provide evidence of this and of the classical nature of the formula. See also C. Spicq, 'L'exégèse de Hébr. XI:1 par S. Thomas', *RSPhTh* 31 (1947), 229-236.

33 See Acts 2:41; 6:7; 12:24; 19:20; 1 Pet 1:23-25. See also R. Schnackenburg, *The Church and the New Testament* (London, 1974), pp. 43-46.

34 References to my *Vraie et fausse réforme* (Paris, 1950), pp. 422-423, 424 note 32, 504-505; 2nd ed. (1969), pp. 344 and 367. For a historical account of Luther's beliefs and interventions concerning the ecclesiological question, see H. Strohl, *La Pensée de la Réforme* (Neuchâtel and Paris, 1951), pp. 173-188.

35 *Luthers Vorlesung über den Hebräerbrief*, ed. E. Hirsch and H. Rückert (Berlin and Leipzig, 1929), p. 1929. Christ will manifest himself *per visum* (by sight), but here below *per auditum* (by hearing): see Luther's *Dict. super Psalt.* (*WA* 3, 628, 1-13; 4, 8, 3235 and 403, 14-26).

36 Augustine, *Enarr. in Ps.* 44, 23 (*PL* 36, 508), cited in the Decree of Vatican II on the Church's Missionary Activity, *Ad Gentes* 1.

37 See Lk 8:11; 1 Pet 1:23-25; 1 Jn 3:9, which some commentators such as C. H.

Dodd and F. Porsch interpret as the word and others such as Raymond Brown and R. Schnackenburg as the Holy Spirit.

38 Augustine, *Enarr. in Ps.* 40, 1 (*PL* 36, 453).

39 *Ibid.*, 30, 4 (*PL* 36, 232).

40 See *Tradition and Traditions, op. cit.* (note 23), pp. 196-206.

41 Pius XII, Allocution *Animus noster*, for the centenary of the Gregorian University, 17 October 1953: see *AAS* 45 (1953), 685. The formula *sibi est fons* is found in F. Dieckmann, *De Ecclesia* (Freiburg, 1925), II, p. 670 and in A. Deneffe, *Der Traditionsprinzip. Studie zur Theologie* (Münster, 1931), pp. 147-148. For my rejection, see *Tradition and Traditions, op. cit.*, pp. 205-206.

42 See *Tradition and Traditions, op. cit.*, pp. 346-347; see also pp. 120ff.

43 Historical and iconological documentation will be found in Romeo de Maio, *The Book of the Gospels at the Oecumenical Councils* (Vatican City, 1963), a very substantial and instructive work. The book of the Gospels was placed on the chair of St Augustine for the unforgettable ceremony on the eve of Pentecost 1982 with John Paul II and Archbishop Runcie at Westminster.

44 See 1 Cor 12:3; 1 Jn 4:2-3; Rev 19:10.

45 In addition to the references offered in support of this conclusion in *Tradition and Traditions, op. cit.*, p. 346, see also A. Feuillet, 'De munere doctrinali a Paraclito in Ecclesia expleto iuxta Evangelium S. Ioannis', *De Scriptura et Traditione* (Rome, 1963), pp. 115-136. See also *I Believe in the Holy Spirit, op. cit.* (note 16) I, pp. 57-59 and II, pp. 5-49.

46 J. H. Newman, *Fifteen Sermons Preached before the University of Oxford* (new ed., London, 1884), pp. 313-314.

47 Are references really necessary here? The theme is found throughout the Gospel of John: see 1:18; 3:11-13, 31-36; 5:19-23; 7:17; 8:26, 28, 38; 12:49-50; 14:10.

48 I. de la Potterie, 'La notion de témoignage dans saint Jean', *Sacra Pagina* II (Paris and Gembloux, 1959), pp. 193-208: 'It is the Spirit who makes the truth of Christ known and thereby arouses faith'.

49 See *WA* 7, 546. There is a clear echo here of personal experience. Luther's text continues: 'Where one has experienced that he is a God who looks at those who are furthest from him and that he comes to the help of those who are poor, condemned, wretched and nothing at all ...'.

50 *Commentary on Galatians* (1519) (*WA* 2, 509, 14-15). We know that elsewhere the sacraments are joined to the Word, especially when the object of ministry is involved: see the Augsburg Confession, 5 and 7. But how many times does Luther say that the Church is constituted by the Word and that it is the Word that does everything! See my study 'Les deux formes du Pain de vie dans l'Evangile et dans la Tradition', *Parole de Dieu et Sacerdoce* (Paris, 1962), pp. 21-58, especially pp. 36f.

51 Schmalkaldic Articles (1537), III, 8: *Bekenntnisschriften* (Göttingen, 1952), pp. 453-454; see also *WA* 50, 245ff. See also P. Fraenkel, 'Le Saint Esprit dans l'enseignement et la prédication de Luther, 1538-1546', F. J. Leenhardt *et al.*, *Le Saint-Esprit* (Geneva, 1963), pp. 59-84.

52 References in *I Believe in the Holy Spirit, op. cit.*, I, p. 141; texts p. 148. Here I

cite merely Théo Preiss, *Le témoignage intérieur du Saint-Esprit* (*Cahiers Théologiques* 13; Neuchâtel and Paris, 1946). See also W. Kreck, *op. cit.* (note 17).

53 Preiss, *op. cit.*

54 Dogmatic Constitution on the Church, *Dei Verbum* 8.

55 R. Marlé, *Introduction to Hermeneutics* (London and New York, 1967).

56 *Tradition and Traditions*, *op. cit.* (note 23), pp. 469-482. Since then the proceedings of the Montreal Conference have been published: *World Conference on Faith and Order* (London and New York, 1964). It is interesting to compare the preparatory reports of the American and the European sections. They are to be found in *Verbum caro* XVII, no. 68 (1963), 371-442. A study of this question has been written by B. Grybba, *The Tradition. An Ecumenical Breakthrough? A Study of Faith and Order Study* (Rome, 1971). The great commentary on *Dei Verbum*, published under the direction of B. D. Dupuy in the collection *Unam Sanctam* (nos 70a and b; Paris, 1968) includes a comparison of chapter II of this Constitution and the Montreal text by J.-L. Leuba, pp. 475-497. G. G. Blum, *Offenbarung and Überlieferung. Die dogmatische Konstitution Dei Verbum des II Vatikanums im Lichte altkirchlicher und moderner Theologie* (Göttingen, 1971), also offers a comparison of the teaching of the Council, not only with the Fathers, but also with Montreal and contemporary Protestant theologians. It is very positive.

57 These texts are to be found in A. Ganoczy's excellent book, *Calvin, théologien de l'Eglise et du ministère* (*Unam Sanctam* 48; Paris, 1964). See especially Calvin's commentary on Eph 4:11-12, *Commentaire sur le Nouveau Testament* (Edition de la Société Calviniste de la France, IV; Geneva, 1965), pp. 193-194 and 196-197: 'Hence one may clearly perceive that they are usually mad, those who without this means think that they can become perfect in Christ. How fantastic are those who manufacture for themselves secret revelations of the Holy Spirit and those proud individuals to whom it seems quite permissible to read Scripture in private, so that they have no need of the common ministry of the Church! For it is the task of Christ alone to instruct the Church and it is for him alone to ordain the means of edification as he may wish. And St Paul clearly bears witness here that, in accordance with the order laid down by Christ, we are not perfect as we should be perfect and we are placed together other than by external preaching, when we allow ourselves to be governed and taught by men'.

58 Let me give a few references among many possible ones: B. Zenowski, 'La "sobornost" dans la nature de l'homme', *DViv* 27 (1956), 91-194; Y. Congar, 'The Human Person and Human Liberty in Oriental Anthropology' (Fr. orig. 1952), in *Dialogue between Christians* (London and Dublin, 1966), pp. 232-245; *idem*, 'Une pneumatologie ecclésiologique', *Initiation à la pratique de la théologie* II (Paris, 1982), pp. 483-516; Carlo Molari, 'The Hermeneutical Rôle of the Christian Community on the Basis of Judaeo-Christian Experience', *Concilium* 113 (1978), 93-105.

59 See the Dogmatic Constitution on the Church, *Dei Verbum* 10, 2.

60 To give only one example (and one from the past), the criteria used to establish whether the Immaculate Conception of Mary could be defined as revealed would seem to fall well short of our present demands. See G. Thils, 'La définition de

l'Immaculée Conception et l'idée de Révélation', *EThL* 31 (1955), 34-45; E. Schillebeeckx, *Revelation and Theology* (London, 1967), p. 173.

61 See my *Un peuple messianique. L'Eglise, sacrement du salut. Salut et libération* *(Cogitatio fidei* 85; Paris, 1975), pp. 70ff. See also p. 34 note 16 for references to the sacraments as proceeding from the Incarnation.

62 *I Believe in the Holy Spirit, op. cit.* (note 16), III, pp. 250-257.

63 Dogmatic Consitution on the Liturgy, *Sacrosanctum Concilium* 7, 2.

4

The Spirit and truth
The Spirit is truth

The Paraclete or Holy Spirit is called the 'Spirit of truth' (see Jn 14:17; 15:26; 16:13; 1 Jn 4:6). We are also told that 'the Spirit is the truth' (1 Jn 5:7). Many studies have sought to define the concept of 'truth' assumed in the texts produced in the Johannine circle. Most distinguish between a 'Greek' and a 'biblical' concept of truth and some go so far as to oppose these two ideas. The former is understood in relation to what things are in themselves and consists of a revelation of what they are. The Greek word *alētheia* is formed from the privative *a-* combined with the root *lēth*, to be hidden. The knowledge that we have 'is true', as is the formula in which we express that knowledge. This meaning is not unknown in Scripture[1] and it would be simplistic to overlook it.

Nevertheless, it is impossible not to recognize the distinctiveness of the biblical concept. The Hebrew word for truth is *'emeth*, derived from the verb *'āman*, which means to be stable, firm, sure, reliable. What is stable, then, 'is true'. Of the 132 times that the word is used in the Old Testament, more than half refer to God. Studies of the biblical concept of 'truth' therefore almost always have, for internal reasons, to end by speaking about God and his attributes.[2] This is of decisive importance for the notion of truth contained in the Bible and for the quality of the truth to which it refers.

On the one hand, God is the first true one because he is the first one who is stable, firm, faithful and reliable: 'Know therefore that the Lord your God is God, the faithful (true) God (*'āman*), who keeps covenant and steadfast love with those who love him . . . to a thousand generations' (Dt 7:9). In the book of Revelation, the victorious Christ is called 'Faithful and True' (Rev 19:11; cf. 1:5; 3:7, 14). God has this attribute because he *is*. The revelation of his name to Moses (Ex 3:14) has in the past been translated, notably in the Septuagint and the Vulgate, as 'I am (the one) who am', but it is now widely accepted that a better translation is that followed by the *Traduction oecuménique de la Bible*, namely, 'I am who I shall be'. The faithfulness of God, then, his 'truth' and stability, is based on what he is. It is identical with his being and his being is that of the 'living God' who has freely shaped a plan of self-communication and salvation.[3] He is, in other words, the God who is called in the book of Revelation 'the one who is, who was and who is to come' (Rev 1:4, 8; 4:8; cf. 11:17; 16:5).

On the other hand, however, there is another aspect of truth that is very similar to this. The truth which is based on God and which he communicates to his Word as a quality and in the self-revelation of his Word as its content is the truth and faithfulness of his plan of grace. That is why the Second Vatican Council proclaimed in its Dogmatic Constitution *Dei Verbum* on Divine Revelation that 'the books of Scripture must be acknowledged as teaching firmly, faithfully and without error that *truth* which God wanted put into the sacred writings *for the sake of our salvation*' (11, 2). The words that I have italicized have been stressed and commented on by many writers.[4]

The truth communicated by the Bible, then, is that of God's plan of grace invested in the facts and the words that have been handed down to us. The book of Genesis is neither a cosmological nor a palaeontological work. It is the first chapter of the history of our salvation. I think Karl Barth was right when he said that everything can be seen from the end onwards, that end being our communion in Christ, aimed at in the decree of election which set everything in motion, and creation itself. It is possible to say that the last two chapters of the book of Revelation render an account of the first two chapters of Genesis. The end, in the sense of finality, determines the form and is what God's plan and the Bible, which reveals that plan, have in view. 'The thought of the Bible is directed towards destinies rather than towards essences' (Dupuy and Chenu; see below, note 4). The language of the Bible is eschatological and expresses what things and men are called to be according to God's plan.

That is why the Word, which expresses the will of God, is addressed, in man, to the mind and to the 'heart'. What prevents man from hearing that Word is not weakness of intelligence, but hardness of heart and rational pride: 'I thank thee, Father, Lord of heaven and earth, that thou hast hidden these things from the wise and understanding and revealed them to babes' (Mt 11:25). The reply that the martyr Theophilus of Antioch gave to the pagan who asked him 'Show me your God' was: 'Show me your man and I will show you my God. Present, while seeing, the eyes of your soul and, while listening, the ears of your heart'.[5]

It is, I think, in this perspective that we have to understand the words of Jesus, which are almost meaningless in the Greek sense: 'He who does what is true comes to the light . . . ' (Jn 3:21). This is parallel to what is found in the Hebrew scriptures, namely, 'walking in the truth'[6] and even 'doing what is true'.[7] The words 'in mercy' are often added to 'in the truth' and this can be understood as living in accordance with the faithfulness of the God of the covenant. What is said of the faithful person is true of the Church as a whole. Hence those astonishing words in the Dogmatic Constitution *Dei Verbum* of Vatican II, which could hardly have entered the minds of the Fathers of the First Vatican Council: *Ecclesia, volventibus saeculis, ad plenitudinem divinae veritatis iugiter tendit, donec in ipsa consummentur verba Dei*, 'As the centuries succeed one another, the Church constantly moves forward towards the fullness of divine truth until the words of God reach their complete fulfilment in her' (8, 2). The 'fullness of truth' is, of course, eschatological. The same Dogmatic Constitution also says that 'the deeds wrought by God in the history of salvation manifest and confirm *doctrinam et res verbis significatas*, the teaching and realities signified by the words' (*Dei Verbum* 2). P. Smulders, commenting on this, insisted that the word *res*, translated here as 'realities', should be understood in the sense in which the same word is used of the sacraments, that is, as the spiritual fruit towards which they are directed.[8]

One remarkable aspect of the Constitution is its Christological orientation. Christ Jesus is the fullness of the Word of God. The opening verses of the letter to the Hebrews say as much and the fourth gospel tells us that Jesus is the Word of God made flesh. God's truth–stability–faithfulness, then, is communicated to Jesus, who can consequently say: 'I am the way, and the truth, and the life' (Jn 14:6). This declaration of identity, one of the seven appearances in this gospel of *egō eimi*, 'I am', has been studied and discussed by Ignace de la Potterie,[9] who has pointed out that the most important of these three concepts is *hodos*, 'way', and this is explicitated by the words 'truth' and 'life', which make clear the sense in which or the reason why Jesus is the way. As the context indicates, he is the way towards the Father insofar as he is the truth and the life — the truth and therefore the life. He is the way because he comes from the Father and because he is sent by him. Men can go up again through him (in him!) to the Father because he has come from the Father to them. He is truth as the incarnate one and he is total, definitive, ultimate and eschatological truth: 'The hour is coming, and now is, when the true worshippers will worship the Father in spirit and truth' (Jn 4:23). Walking in the truth had, in the old order, a psychological and moral character. With the sending of Jesus and his Spirit, it became in a much more decisive way a sharing in the truth and stability of God, in other words, of the Father. Jesus[10] reveals what the Father has taught him (8:28) and what he has heard from the Father (8:26). He speaks about what he has seen with the Father (3:11; 8:38), he does what he has seen the Father do (5:19) and he 'bears witness to what he has seen and heard' (3:32).

The Spirit is totally relative to Jesus. His coming is linked to the departure and the absence, in a certain sense, of Jesus, to the extent that it is good that Jesus should go away (16:7). His activity is relative to the truth that Jesus was and is. He 'brings to remembrance' what Jesus has said (14:26). He 'bears witness' to Jesus (15:26). He will guide us into (*hodēgēsai*) the whole truth (6:13), that is, he will make us take the way (*hodos*) of truth and life that Jesus is and that his words are, because they are 'spirit and life' (6:63). The Spirit too is truth, both in his relationship with the incarnate Word and also because he also comes from the Father and Jesus sends him from the Father (15:26).

But how can the Spirit be and do this in history, the time of Jesus' corporeal absence? This is indicated to us in the New Testament in three ways especially:

(1) The Spirit will be *with* the disciples and even *in* them *eis ton aiōna*, for ever. He will be with and in them as the Spirit of truth in order to bear witness with them to Christ and his work (Jn 15:26-27). Even more striking is the text in which John speaks of the witness borne by the Spirit by affirming that 'the Spirit is the truth' and goes on to say: 'There are three witnesses, the Spirit, the water and the blood; and these three agree', in other words, they bear a single witness (1 Jn 5:7-8). One possible way of interpreting this is that the water signifies baptism and the blood the Eucharist,[11] although the context is Christological. The Spirit is mentioned first because he brings about the faith that is a precondition for the other two. Baptism and the Eucharist make the Church. They are relative to Christ and bring him into the heart of the world as the principle of life.

(2) The Acts of the Apostles make us acquainted, in a way that is admittedly reconstructed and schematic, with the life of the apostolic Church. This is putting into practice what Jesus declared: 'When the Counsellor (Paraclete) comes, whom I shall send to you from the Father, even the Spirit of truth, who proceeds from the Father, he will bear witness to me; and you also are witnesses, because you have been with me from the beginning' (Jn 15:26-27). This promise is echoed by Peter and the apostles when they declare to the Sanhedrin: 'We are witnesses to these things (*rhēmatōn*) and so is the Holy Spirit whom God has given to those who obey him' (Acts 5:32). The apostolic Church was in fact a real and active 'concelebration' with the Holy Spirit.[12] Finally, according to Revelation, the book in which the future of that same apostolic Church is unveiled, 'the testimony of Jesus is the spirit of prophecy' (Rev 19:10). This book also closes with an appeal to the eschatological Christ: 'The Spirit and the Bride say, "Come!" ' (22:17).

(3) Revelation also speaks of the historical life of the Church that is to come as a struggle against the Beast — the Power that is opposed to the rule of God — and the False Prophet — the distortion of the gospel of Christ, possibly even by members of the People of God. This situation is already proclaimed in the passages in the fourth gospel concerning the Paraclete: the world is unable to receive the Spirit of truth (14:17) because God's adversary, the spirit of the lie, the Demon, dwells and works in it (see 8:44). A great trial takes place throughout the history of the world, a trial for or against Jesus.

God, who decided in favour of Jesus by raising him from the dead, sends the Spirit, the Paraclete, to the disciples to strengthen them by reassuring them that the world is wrong and the one who inspires it is already confounded and condemned (see 16:8-11).[13] The witness borne by the Christian consists in being united with Jesus Christ who was accused because he was opposed to the world and in being united with his victory, by passing through a struggle, in which the help of the Paraclete is assured.

In the inspired Johannine synthesis, the truth goes from God to God, passing through the incarnate Word and the people of God. God the Father is true, authentic, stable, in his very being. His eternal Word is true because it is his Word. It became flesh in Jesus Christ and was communicated to men through him and his Spirit. By receiving and keeping the Word and the Spirit, we can walk (2 Jn 4; 3 Jn 3 and 4), have grace and truth (2 Jn 1-3), love (1 Jn 3:18), be consecrated (Jn 17:17, 19), worship (4:23) and be free (8:32) in truth or in the truth. We can, in a word, live truly.

There are, then, as it were two levels of existence. The first is the purely 'carnal' life, lived at the purely biological and psychical level according to this world. The second is the true existence, Augustine's *vere esse*, the eschatological life of which I have been speaking in this chapter. Benefiting from this level of existence is salvation. The book of Revelation describes that truth and we can only seize hold of it thanks to the Spirit, who alone knows what there is in God (see 1 Cor 2:9-16).

Notes

1   See, for example, 1 Kings 10:6: what had been reported to the Queen of Sheba was true. Micaiah is commanded to tell the truth: 1 Kings 22:16 (cf. Jer 9:5[4]; Zech 8:16). In Jn 5:33, the meaning is above all juridical. For the value of agreement with reality in the biblical concept of '*emeth*, see D. Mêhel, 'Ämät. Untersuchungen über "Wahrheit" im Hebräischen', *ABG* XII, 1 (Bonn, 1968), pp. 30-57.

2   This is true, for example, of E. T. Ramsdell, 'The Old Testament Understanding of Truth', *JR* 31 (1951), 264-273; and of K. Alanen, 'Das Wahrheitsproblem in der Bibel und in der griechischen Philosophie', *KuD* 3 (1957), 230-239.

3   The uses of the biblical term draw attention especially to the power of God and the indestructible nature of what he does. See J. Guillet, 'Le titre biblique Le Dieu Vivant', *L'homme devant Dieu. Mélanges offerts au Père H. de Lubac* I (*Théologie* 56; Paris, 1963), pp. 11-23. In the New Testament, the living God communicates life or his life.

4   See I. de la Potterie, 'La vérité de la Sainte Ecriture et l'Histoire du salut d'après la constitution dogmatique Dei Verbum', *NRT* 88 (1966), 151-169. J. Coppens' criticisms in *Acta Cong. Intern. de Theologia Concilii Vaticani* II (Vatican, 1968), pp. 545f. have not led me to question de la Potterie's interpretation. See also B.

D. Dupuy, *Vatican II. La Révélation divine (Unam Sanctam* 70b; Paris, 1968), pp. 563-566. M.-D. Chenu's observations are very indicative: 'Vérité évangélique et métaphysique wolffienne à Vatican II', *RSPhTh* 57 (1975), 632-640.

5 Theophilus of Antioch, *Ad Autolycum* I, 2 (*SC* 20 [1968], pp. 60-63; *PG* 6, 1025). Similar texts can be found in my *Tradition and Traditions* (London and New York, 1966), pp. 254-255 note 2.

6 See Is 38:3; Pss 26:3; 86:11; 1 Kings 2:4; 3:6; 2 Kings 20:3; Tob 3:5 [RSV has 'faithfulness' in most of these passages].

7 See Tob 4:6; 13:6; 2 Chron 31:20; Sir 27:9.

8 Cited by H. du Lubac in *Vatican II. La Révélation divine* I (*Unam Sanctam* 70a; Paris, 1968), p. 179 note 13. See also M.-D. Chenu, *op. cit.*, 638.

9 I. de la Potterie, ' "Je suis la Voie, la Vérité et la Vie" (Jn 14, 6)', *NRT* 88 (1966), 907-943, repr. in *La vérité selon S. Jean* (Rome, 1977).

10 Jn 14:16-17; the *Traduction oecuménique* [and JB, NJB, unlike RSV] follows the manuscripts which have the present tense: 'He dwells with you and *is* in you'. F. Porsch, *Pneuma und Wort. Ein exegetischer Beitrag zur Pneumatologie des Johannesevangeliums* (Frankfurt, 1974), pp. 244ff., gives his reasons for likewise following the present tense, but referring it to 'the time of the Church'

11 See A. Feuillet in *De Scriptura et Traditione* (Rome, 1963), pp. 115-136; F. M. Braun; F. Porsch, *op. cit.*, pp. 336-337, with reference to Jn 19:34.

12 See my study, cited several times by Paul VI: *RSPhTh* 36 (1952), 613-625, and 37 (1953), 24-48; trans. as 'The Holy Spirit and the Apostolic Body, Continuators of the Work of Christ', *The Mystery of the Church* (London, 1960), pp. 147-186.

13 See M.-F. Berrouard, 'Le Paraclet, défenseur du Christ devant la conscience du croyant', *RSPhTh* 33 (1949), 361-389. See also the notes in JB [and NJB].

5

Autonomy of the Spirit?

Catholic ecclesiology, especially as it has been expounded since the Council of Trent, has been been based on the conviction that Christ founded a Church — *his* Church, *the* Church — as a hierarchically structured society provided with all the means needed for its mission to communicate salvation. This was at least the predominant pattern until the renewal on which Vatican II set the seal. The encyclical *Mystici Corporis* of 29 June 1943 contributed a number of important additional spiritual values to this outline, but did not replace it. Christ continued to be regarded above all as the founder of the Church.

This ecclesiology was predisposed to place within the institution and even within the hands of the clergy a reserve of the means of grace, readily available and only needing to be used. It would be hard to refrain from repeating Möhler's summing up in 1823 of the ecclesiology that had been presented to him: 'God founded the hierarchy and in that action provided for everything that was needed until the end of time'.

I have myself said often enough that we should not minimize the importance of those spiritual movements which are to a greater or lesser degree opposed to hierarchical structures, sacramentarianism, the domination of the clergy and sometimes of the secular lords, and which have proliferated from the beginning of the eleventh century onwards.[1] Although these movements are very different from each other — Catharism, for example, calls for a special assessment — they have one thing in common: they all share a desire to escape from the establishment of a power structure and to derive an evangelical way of life directly from the sources, not through the mediation of clergy.

These desires appeared in a radical form in the sixteenth century. The Reformers did not exclude the foundation of the Church by Christ or the mediation of the word, the sacraments and the ministry. They did, however, emphasize very strongly the action here and now of God in justification and in the whole process of salvation. There was no kind of reserve of the means of grace that simply had to be put to use. God himself builds up his Church, first of all by his Word and then by the active faith that he arouses in the souls of believers. Within a Church, with its ministers and its sacraments, there was a direct relationship of faith with the Word of God. The term 'private interpretation' is very controversial and in any case of later date, but it does point, if clumsily, to this state of immediacy and personal relationship.

Christian thought and action resulting from the Reformation has undoubtedly produced in the past four centuries a fantastic burgeoning of initiatives, movements and even new 'churches'. If this is viewed from the vantage-point of the Tridentine and post-Tridentine Church, an almost endless 'history of variations' could be written, but it is also possible to look at this history in a different way. I would suggest that we should begin by not applying any ecclesiological criteria at first, in order simply to see what has happened.

There have been — there always are — vertical interventions here and now by God in the lives of men. It would be presumptuous of me to claim to be writing a history of these. A few mentions will be sufficient,[2] taken from the Christian world deriving from the Reformation, though I could equally well have compiled items from the history of the Catholic Church.

George Fox (1624-91) went so far as to reject all the sacraments and all church organization, so convinced was he by the evidence of the 'inner light'. Christ had for too long been enclosed in the Mass or in the Bible. He should be our prophet, our priest and our king, and we should obey him. His movement led to the creation of the remarkable Society of Friends or Quakers.

The Pietist movement began as a reaction against Lutheran orthodoxy that was too certain of its formulae and its authority. It stressed rebirth, personal faith and spiritual experience. Philipp Jakob Spener, whose *Pia Desideria* appeared in 1675, set up in his own home or in those of his followers basic communities known as *collegia pietatis*, to whose members he repeated, as a kind of charter for Christian life, the admonition of St Paul: 'Let the Word of Christ dwell in you richly, as you teach and admonish one another in all wisdom, and sing psalms and hymns and spiritual songs with thankfulness in your hearts to God' (Col 3:16).

It is interesting to note how fruitful this and other spiritual movements were, especially in their encouragement of new initiatives. One of the most important of these was taken by Nikolaus Ludwig, Graf von Zinzendorf (1700-60), who was brought up in Pietism and converted as a young man to the cause of Christ, in his foundation and protection of a new community of Moravian Brethren on one of his estates, known as Herrnhut, from 1722 onwards.

Here, for example, is a description of what happened at Herrnhut during a celebration of the Lord's Supper on 13 August 1727. According to a witness, Arvid Gravin, 'they were so moved that their hearts burned with a new love and with great faith in the Saviour as well as with fervent love for each other. This discomposed them to such a degree that they wept and threw themselves into each others' arms and that holy unity increased among them, almost as if the unity that had existed among the earlier Moravian Brethren had risen from the ashes'. Although they were few in number, these new Moravian Brethren undertook many missions. They had contact with their Brethren in Georgia and later in England and this played a part in the vocation of John Wesley, who even went to Herrnhut to confirm his own feelings.

The great adventure of Methodism began with Wesley. Here, as with all similar vocations, a direct experience of God was at the source, in this case felt, on 24 May 1738, as an experience of warmth. Later, on 1 January 1739, also following a celebration of the Lord's Supper, this time in London, 'at about three o'clock in the morning, while we were continuing to pray, the presence of God came down on us with such force that many of us uttered cries, suffering from an excess of joy. There were also some who fell to the ground. As soon as we had recovered a little from our terror and astonishment at the presence of the Lord, we cried out with a single voice: We praise you, O God! We know that you are the Lord!'. Methodism has nourished the lives of countless believers. The Holiness Churches in the United States were originally connected with it, even though they left it and have since been affected by other movements.

Britain and America have been particularly marked by a number of revivals, although they do not have a monopoly of these. Certain times seem to be ripe for religious revivals, but all such movements begin with a person whose soul is seized by God and who dedicates himself to the absolute service of God's sovereignty. Jonathan Edwards (1703-58) was such a man. He went, with George Whitefield (1714-70), to New England in 1740 and was the artisan of the 'Great Awakening' of Northampton, Mass.[3] This had already begun in 1733, when 'the Spirit of God was beginning to work in an extraordinary way'. God had invaded Edwards's life on 12 January 1723. He himself says that he solemnly made a gift of himself to God in writing: 'I have been before God, and have given myself, all that I am and have, to God; so that I am not, in any respect, my own' (*Diary*).

I do not intend to provide an account here of all these revivals, but it is worth mentioning the Welsh revival of 1738-42 and Howell Harris (1714-73), who had a profound experience at Pentecost in 1735, again after a celebration of the Lord's Supper, when his 'heart was burning with the fire of the love of God'.

And what am I to say about such movements in the United States of America, which is above all the country of personal initiatives? I will mention only one event, which took place in the school of biblical studies in Topeka, Kansas and was, I think, the source of the American movement of Renewal in the Spirit. Those at the school in 1900 had been studying the Acts of the Apostles, and they wondered why what was reported in that book no longer happened. Then, on 1 January 1901, Agnes Ozment had the following experience:

> On the first day of 1901, the Lord was present with us in a remarkable way, calming down our hearts in order to let them aspire to greater things. In the evening, the Spirit of prayer came over us. It was almost eleven o'clock when the longing came to me, asking for hands to be laid on me so that I might receive the gift of the Holy Spirit. As soon as hands had been laid on my head, the Holy Spirit fell on me and I began to speak in tongues, glorifying God. It was as if rivers of living water were rising up from the depths of my being.

The birth of the Pentecostal Movement and its rapid spread across the United States from 1906 onwards are well known. After remaining a marginal phenomenon in the great classical churches, it began to penetrate them — the Protestant churches from 1956 and Catholicism from January 1967 onwards. Here too, I shall limit myself to a few significant examples, so as to provide a foundation for a number of general comments. It would not be difficult to find examples in the lives of Catholic men and women, since the recent history of the Renewal is full of them, but I have said enough and will add only one more instance, a very fruitful one, namely Africa.

Africa is a continent where sects and churches are always springing up. As many as 8,600 have recently been counted. Some of these groups are formed by secession from one of the classical churches, which are often regarded as having acted as vehicles of the evil of colonialism. Others form themselves around a charismatic and inspired person who speaks on the strength of a personal experience or a personal understanding of the Bible. Clive Dillon-Malone has called these sects 'Spirit Churches'.[4]

I have been able to check the exactitude of the profile that he provides of the calling of a founder of such a sect in the story of the founder of the Church of Heavenly Christianity, Samuel Biléou Joseph Oschoffa.[5] The principal elements are: a disappearance into a strange and difficult world, yet a climate of intense prayer, followed by a reappearance comparable to a return to life; a vision, accompanied by the revelation of a special calling, which gives rise to opposition; the gifts of healing and preaching; the creation of a 'church' with the hero as 'Prophet–Pastor–Founder'. Great importance is attached to the Bible and verses from the Old and New Testament are frequently quoted. There is an intense prayer life and the life of the church and its worship are organized in detail. This is certainly not to be despised: it has great spiritual substance, in spite of the lack of eucharistic reality, which has, in my opinion, been really betrayed. And one question that arises at once in this context is: Where is the unity of the Church of Christ in this multiplicity of inspirations?

From these data there arise a few general comments. Although each case is original in itself, there is often a relationship between them in that they encourage each other's development and follow each other's example. They often begin in similar ways. This is clear, I think, today in the case of the Renewal. It is possible to discover a shared element at the level of their historical context. They all come about, in other words, in a spirit of reaction or revolt against a climate of rationality or even rationalism, a climate in which religion has become too reasonable or has come to conform too closely to the wishes of the world. This would explain why the classical churches are so often apathetic towards the sects, as happened, I think, in England and New England in the eighteenth century. And has the Christianity produced by the African missions not been felt by the people of those countries as something externally regulated and imposing forms originating in the rationality of the Western world?

The data of which I have given instances point clearly to two lines of action in God's work which can be called the way of mediation and the way of immediacy. In both cases, it is God doing his work and building up or giving life to his Church. He does not, however, only do it through the means instituted as a result of the work of the incarnate Word. He also intervenes directly in individual lives.

This can be seen quite clearly in the gospels and in Acts. In the first place, there is the way of *mediation*. A text which comes to mind at once is: 'He who receives you receives me, and he who receives me receives him who sent me' (Mt 10:40). Then there are the texts on the 'power of the keys' (Mt 16:19; 18:17-18; Jn 20:22-23). The Acts of the Apostles include such texts as: 'You will be told what you are to do' (9:6); 'God ... made him manifest, not to all the people, but to us who were chosen by God as witnesses ... And he commanded us to preach to the people and to testify ... ' (10:40-42); 'And they (Paul and Barnabas) appointed elders ... in every church' (14:23). Other texts can be found in the epistles: Eph 4:11-16; Tit 1:5; Jas 5:14 and 16, etc.

These are no more than examples. But there are also texts and instances of *immediacy*. Ananias had to baptize Paul, but Christ had appeared to Paul beforehand. The Holy Spirit had already 'fallen on' Cornelius and his family before Peter commanded them to be baptized (Acts 10:44-48). During the apostolic age, there were several recorded revelations of the mystery of salvation coming directly from heaven (see, for example, Gal 1:11, 16; Eph 3:3, 5). It is, moreover, not possible to make a sharp contrast between immediacy and mediation, since quite often one way is contained within the other or added to it, usually when God intervenes directly in an existing structure and a visible ministry (see, for example, Acts 1:15-26; 1 Tim 4:14; 2 Tim 1:6; 1 Pet 4:10-11).

Initiatives like the examples I have cited are not entirely divorced from the instituted means of grace. There are, as we have seen, several cases of inner illumination that have occurred during prayer following the celebration of the Lord's Supper. In almost every case too, the Bible plays a crucial part. Clearly, an irreducible personal factor enters into the instituted framework, but this does not mean that it is not Christological. It could be called an element of Christological pneumatology or pneumatological Christology.

In this context, we are reminded of Paul's statement: 'Now the Lord is the Spirit, and where the Spirit of the Lord is, there is freedom' (2 Cor 3:17). Christ, in other words, is living and active! He intervenes! In the Pauline text I have just quoted, the free action of the Lord, the Spirit, refers to a Christological interpretation of Scripture, but the work of Christ in history cannot be reduced to what has been instituted in the constitutive history of biblical revelation and the incarnation.

This is a question of monumental proportions, which can be broken down into several individual parts. There is in the first place the question of personal initiative. This is an indisputable reality which cannot be overlooked and which is not expressed in a Catholicism consisting purely of organization and obedience. Then we have to consider in what sense revelation is closed and in what sense it is not. The Spirit blows where he will. Jesus compared the Spirit to the wind — we are aware that it can move things, but we do not know where it comes from or where it goes. Is there a completely emancipated freedom with regard to the revealed and instituted economy of salvation? Have we to look not only in the direction of the Holy Spirit and his freedom, but also in that of a pneumatological Christology, and in what sense is the Spirit the Spirit of Christ? Finally, is this sense restricted purely to the economy or does it extend as far as the level of 'theology', in other words of the eternal Trinitarian mystery?

Each question must be discussed in turn, though not all need to be developed at the same length.

Personal initiative

Some things are codified, some are experienced. There are official or agreed texts, and there is reality. At the latter level there have been and still are many initiatives, cases of resistance to abstract rules — in other words, cases of personal vitality. Until the fairly recent past, however, there was, it seemed, only one virtue — obedience — and only one sin — that of the 'flesh'.[6]

The explosion caused by Luther's revolt and its far-reaching consequences made the Catholic Church insist to the point of nervous tension on obedience to authority. This can be felt in Leo X's Bull *Exsurge Domine* of 15 June 1520: *Nervum ecclesiasticae disciplinae, obedientiam scilicet quae fons est et origo omnium virtutum*, '...the strength of the Church's discipline, that is, obedience, which is the source and origin of all virtues...'.[7] A mystique of obedience was set in motion in the Church by Cardinal Caraffa during the pontificate of Paul III in the sixteenth century and continued by him when he became Paul IV and then by Pius IV and Pius V.

This emphasis on obedience is, of course, a prominent aspect of the Tridentine spirit as it is described by G. Alberigo, or in our time of the 'monophorism' described and defined by Maurice Blondel.[8] Everything in the Church that does not conform to strict obedience to authority, identified in practice with that of the Pope or Rome, is branded as 'private interpretation' or rationalism. This is very eloquently illustrated in the work of that eminent Catholic theologian M. J. Scheeben in the nineteenth century and especially in his criticism of the Gallican and Jansenist conception of Tradition, which insisted on the part played in its verification by the early Christian documents and its reception by the churches. According to Scheeben, this was rationalism and private interpretation, an expression of the spirit of the Reformation and naturalism![9] The movement known as Americanism can also be traced back to this origin, insofar as it inclines towards personal initiatives taken within the situation of a 'modern' world recognized and accepted as such.

It would not be difficult to find many denunciations of this situation of passive submission and this failure to recognize at least a marginal area of personal creativity. I shall, however, confine myself to only one example, that of Georges Bernanos: 'The sabotage of that sublime and necessary faculty of the soul known as judgement can only lead to catastrophes... Men trained to blind obedience are those who are also prone to sudden blind disobedience. Obedience without discussion does not in any sense mean the same as obedience without understanding and complete docility is not so very far removed from complete revolt'.[10] This final comment, repeated twice, reminds me of Amiel's observations, which I have cited elsewhere: 'Catholic thought cannot conceive of the personality as master of itself and self-conscious. Its boldness and its weakness spring from the same cause: non-responsibility and the vassalage of the conscience, which knows only slavery or anarchy, which proclaims the law but does not obey it, because the law is outside itself, not within itself'.[11] If we read this text critically, excluding the exaggerations it contains, we can better appreciate how much light it throws on the situation that I have been describing. Insofar as a rule is not internalized and personally appropriated, it will lead either to a passive and external conformity, or to revolt and anarchy. Does the history of many countries that have been influenced by Latin Catholicism not illustrate this?

The problem is that the norms should not become a sort of ready-made straitjacket, sufficient to itself and imposed on people without truly coming to life within them. This would be making man for the sabbath. What is required is that what is done should be the activity of a person, that a person, with his own personal conviction, should be really the subject of that activity. There is, of course, a danger of 'private interpretation', but it is important to examine critically what this category of 'private interpretation', which is employed too easily, really means. We should also be aware of the reality which does not correspond to what has in the past been presented in our apologetics.

The solution is to be found, I think, in an understanding of the Church as a spiritual communion that has a social structure. The term 'communion' implies a conviction or an activity on the part of a person, but it is not the same as individualism. It is, in other words, a question of sharing in the life of a Church, but a Church which is not a purely administrative machine or a power structure with subjugated members. The vitality of such a Church would be put to optimum use in a climate of freedom and trust, in which desiderata and new ideas would have time to mature, to spread through the body of believers without causing damage. If this climate does not exist, if a rigid authority is imposed, insisting on rigorous conformity with what has been habitually accepted, then what is fruitful in the new movement will not be of benefit to the Church, or will only be of benefit much later — or else, the desiderata will ferment and finally lead to breakages.

The Church is not just an establishment where past forms are preserved. It is Tradition, and true Tradition is criticism and creativity as well as the handing-down and preservation of identical realities. One form of Catholicism has failed to express the dimension of hope — and I use the word 'express' advisedly, because this element was there but was not expressed as a theme or a dimension of history. Hope was reserved for the 'last ends' or the spiritual life of the individual. There was an insufficient sense of history. Catholicism appeared orientated towards the past — a past in which an order that was to last for ever had been established. The future is uncertain, and initiatives that point or at least claim to point towards it have too often been viewed with suspicion.

Is revelation closed?

Since the appearance of the Decree *Lamentabili* on 3 July 1907, Catholic treatises *De Revelatione* have had to include a paragraph on the closure of

revelation with the death of the last apostle. The statement that was rejected
was formulated in the following way: *Revelatio, obiectum fidei catholicae
constituans, non fuit cum Apostolis completa*, 'Revelation, which constitutes
the object of Catholic faith, was not completed with the Apostles'.[12] The
Decree was opposed to the idea, suggested by Alfred Loisy, that revelation
was situated in the religious intuitions of humanity, in a perception, growing
and becoming more perfect with time, of the relationship between man and
the unknown God.[13] It also rejected George Tyrrell's mystical view that
revelation appealed to an inner datum, a call or a prophetic message that
continues to be heard in the consciousness of believers.[14] Tyrrell admitted,
however, that the revelation given by Christ and the apostles, independently
of all later theological reflection, already contained everything that was
necessary for the fullness of the life of faith, hope and charity. With the death
of the last apostle, Tyrrell insisted, the regulative and classical period of
Christian inspiration closed, not in the sense that revelation — which is to
some degree a privilege of each man — ceased suddenly, but in the sense that
all later revelation has to be checked and verified in order for it to be brought
into agreement in spirit with the apostolic revelation.[15] This is very close to
the correct position adopted later, for example, by Henri de Lubac, Karl
Rahner and Edward Schillebeeckx, and Loisy was conscious of the difference
between Tyrrell's position and his own.[16]

Various arguments in favour of revelation continuing after the apostolic
period have been put forward throughout the history of Christianity, in
contexts very different from that of modernism. Should Joachim of Fiore be
included in this history? His 'eternal gospel' was a 'spiritual understanding'
of the Old and New Testaments, and so not so much a new revelation as a new
way of interpreting the one revelation and a new way of living it. In his book
with the very general title of 'Joachim of Fiore's spiritual descendants', Henri
de Lubac presents a number of proponents of continuous revelation.[17] Jacob
Böhme (d. 1625) had an experience of light which he attributed to the Spirit
and regarded as completely autonomous with regard to both the Church and
the Bible. There is a personal revelation that is its own Word.[18]

As we know, openness to the idea of a new and creative future can be
transmuted in favour of human reason or nature, as happened especially in
the case of German idealism. In Herder (1744-1803), for example, the
permanent revelation constituted by nature leads to the evaporation of
Christianity.[19]

It is not possible to assimilate to these unacceptable positions the various
uses that have been widely made of the terms *revelare, revelatio* or *inspirare* in
a broader sense by the Church Fathers and in the Middle Ages. Elsewhere I
have provided numerous examples and references to other studies.[20] In
definitions concerning such sacraments as confirmation and the anointing of

the sick; in the definition or formulation of points of doctrine; even in the case of a direction of life, a decision or an appointment to a public function, it used to be habitual to say: 'God has revealed it'. But, with or without a background of Augustinian illumination, 'God has revealed it' in such cases means no more than 'God has enabled it to be understood, discovered or known'. In the past, this was in accordance with an idea that Scripture was sufficient in itself and contained in some way all the truths that were necessary for salvation.[21]

We have honoured Thomas Aquinas in this instance for two reasons. Firstly, he used the term *revelatio* not in the sense of an illumination of the spirit, but in the objective sense, as meaning what is revealed. Secondly, he used it exclusively for public and constitutive supernatural revelation. This use of the word is the one which has prevailed in theology. We have, however, become more sensitive to the more fortunate aspect of the earlier use, which expressed a feeling for the presence here and now of God building up his Church and the fact that the Holy Spirit or Christ pneumatized and in glory is co-existent here and now with the Church of the incarnate Word. Revelation is not closed if the word is understood in the sense that the Church knows the whole content of the Word of God. When Pius XII declared that the bodily Assumption of Mary was *divinitus revelatum dogma*, his statement could only have been made in this sense of 'revelation', namely the revelation that takes place in the Tradition and the life of the Church. Father Malmberg (see below, note 12) has spoken, with reference to such acts on the part of the magisterium, of a 'mediated external revelation' to the Church through the preaching of the apostles and exegesis of the Scriptures. In this case, however, Tradition and the praxis of the Church play a crucial part.

Such classical contemporary theologians as Henri de Lubac,[22] Karl Rahner[23] and Edward Schillebeeckx[24] have explained the idea of the closure of revelation with the death of the last apostle in the sense that the witness borne to Christ, through and in whom the revelation of God's plan and his mystery was fulfilled, was secured and terminated at that moment. It is also certainly in this sense that the Dogmatic Constitution *Dei Verbum* 4 should be understood. This paragraph is very full and it concludes with the statement: 'We now await no further public revelation before the glorious manifestation of our Lord Jesus Christ'.[25]

This clearly leaves the way open for 'private revelations', which concern the historical life of the Church, but not the constitutive articles of apostolic faith.[26] Within the context of these 'private revelations' in the widest sense of the term, it is possible to claim that a charism of special devotion may be equivalent to what Paul calls 'prophecy'. A recent example of this may be Elena Guerra, a religious who was filled with a deep devotion for the Holy Spirit and whose interventions with Leo XIII played an important part in the letters that the latter wrote and promulgated on the subject of the Spirit.[27]

The Second Vatican Council, then, confirmed the idea of a closed revelation, but the competent Commission refused to give way to the request made by Cardinal Ruffini and several bishops to include the formula 'closed at the death of the Apostles'.

It is worth adding that theologians have drawn our attention to the fact, based on the work of exegetes, that the term 'apostle' is applied to others apart from the Twelve in the New Testament.[28] Several even accept that some of the New Testament writings were composed after the death of the apostles, possibly even in the second century A.D. This means that revelation continued throughout the whole of the constitutive period of the Church, insofar as that period included, through God's will, all the canonical Scriptures. The inspired composition of the New Testament, then, formed part of the original constitution of the Church, and the charism of infallibility which follows the inspired character of the Scriptures is consistent with that of the Church.[29]

Institution and charism

The Spirit blows where he will. Is there a freedom of the Spirit with regard to what the Word has affirmed and still affirms? Would any of us be able to reject the excellent question asked by John Ruskin: 'Who knows where it will please God to let down his ladder?' God is free to intervene *ubi et quando* — where and when he pleases. We cannot, however, make that freedom the formula of our ecclesiology without denying the existence of the historical interventions by means of which God has revealed and carried out his plan to constitute a people for himself — his People — within the world.

We may accept this reality, but there remains the question of the relationship between the instituted ministry and the free gifts of the Spirit. The most radical position is that of Rudolf Sohm, who insists that there is absolute opposition or incompatibility between Church and law.[30] The Church of God has only existed, he believes, because of regular interventions throughout history on the part of the Spirit. This construction was disputed by Adolf Harnack, following the discovery and publication of the *Didache* by Mgr Bryennios in 1883. Harnack found in the document the idea of a duality of ministries at the origins of Christianity: a local, instituted, stable ministry, and an itinerant, charismatic one. The existence of this second, charismatic ministry did not, however, stand in the way of a juridical organization of communities — it was added to this, it was something else.

This idea of a duality between instituted functions [in German, *Amt*] and free interventions of the Spirit has persisted until the present, not only as an ever-present problem, but also as a key to the interpretation of the Pauline texts. H. von Campenhausen is one of the many theologians who have considered this question.[31] I do not intend either to outline the history or to provide an account of the debate about the distinction and the relationships between instituted function and charismatic ministry. This has already been done by Ulrich Brockhaus, who, although he has of necessity had to limit it, has provided a very representative and, in that sense, sufficient documentation.[32] It is clear from his analysis that a certain idea of the Church that is linked to confessional options has almost always been taken as a point of departure. Catholics have superimposed on the New Testament texts the idea of a society founded by Christ and consisting of a 'hierarchy' on the basis of a distinction between clergy and laity. Protestants, on the other hand, have unconsciously read St Paul in the light of the incident at Antioch, which has been interpreted as a struggle of the spirit against the institution, or of the prophet against the man of authority. This is based partly on the fact that the word 'charism' or at least its Christian usage originates with St Paul. It also has to do with his being (1) an apostle, not by being instituted as one by the pre-paschal Christ, but by a miraculous intervention by the heavenly Christ, and (2) the theologian of salvation by faith in the gospel, which sets us free from the law and enables us to welcome the Spirit.

It is a mistake to look in the Pauline writings for statements about the constitution of the Church, or even about the organization of churches. Brockhaus has correctly pointed out that the two principal texts — 1 Cor 12 – 14 and Rom 12:1-11 — are both paraenetical or exhortatory. This does not make them in any way less valuable. The Corinthians had put various questions to Paul: on marriage (1 Cor 7:1), on food sacrificed to idols (8:4) and on what they called the *pneumatika* (12:1). In his reply, he defines his own view of the gifts of the Spirit, their function, their assessment and their proper use. God builds up his Church by various ministries, gifts and activities. There is a multiplicity and a great variety of these, but, coming from God, the Lord and the Spirit, their aim is to build up the same organism, the Body of Christ. As they are made 'according to the grace (*charis*) given to us' (Rom 12:6), Paul calls them 'charisms'.

He lists a number of these gifts, although his list does not in any way express the organization of the community (see 1 Cor 12:8-10, 28; Rom 12:6-8; Eph 4:11). He places the gift of being an apostle in the first place, that of being a prophet in the second place, and then the gifts of teaching. The ministries that build up the Body of Christ are above all those of the word that arouses faith, but the communities do have leaders.[33] Paul does not define their status and hardly even describes their function. They are assumed to exist in the communities and it is for the latter that Paul develops his teaching at the level of paraenesis about the proper use of the charisms.[34] Brockhaus notes that Paul, being concerned with paraenesis, is so little interested in organizational structures that it would be as fruitless to look in his letters for definitions of these structures as it would be to try to find signs of opposition to the instituted ministries (*op. cit.* below [note 32], pp. 217 and 239).

Paul therefore develops very precise criteria for the proper use of these charisms and applies these in particular to the two which the Corinthian Christians valued most highly: speaking in tongues and prophecy (1 Cor 14:27-31). These criteria are especially valuable in the building up of the community: charity, peace and good order. This is what makes *pneumatika* into true *charismata* or gifts of grace. All have received them, each one his own gift or gifts. Paul does not stress it, but includes among them those of administration or governing. It is, then, in this way that a community, an *ekklēsia*, is built up which is the Body of Christ, since the gifts of grace make believers into members, each carrying out a function within the body.

Although all this is accomplished by the Spirit, it constitutes not the Body of the Spirit, but that of Christ. The Corinthians were very proud and fond of their *pneumatika* and were very self-confident (see 1 Cor 5:6; 8:9-12). They enjoyed the spiritual gifts so much that they were 'intoxicated' with them (see 1 Cor 15:34 [literally: sober up!]), and greedy for them (14:12). The gifts took the place in their lives of a knowledge of God. As Heinrich Schlier has remarked, Paul contrasted the attitude of the 'enthusiasts' of Corinth with the 'normative paradosis of the indisputable apostolic kerygma . . . the preaching centred on the apostolic tradition'.[35] See 1 Cor 3:5ff.; 4:8, 9. There is no autonomy of pneumatic experience with regard to the Word and therefore with regard to Christ. The confession: 'Jesus is Lord' is a criterion that the Spirit is at work (see 12:3).

It is possible and even necessary to go further in a Christological direction. We have already seen that Paul regarded the Lord as the Spirit (2 Cor 3:17) in the sense that the glorified Jesus acts in the mode of a life-giving spirit (1 Cor 15:45). He and the Spirit work together in such a way that it is possible to attribute the effects of grace either to one or to the other.[36] I very much like the concluding words of the *Gloria*: 'For you alone are the Holy One, you alone are the Most High, Jesus Christ, with the Holy Spirit, in the glory of God the Father'. Jesus has been 'designated Son of God in power according to the Spirit of holiness by his resurrection from the dead' (Rom 1:4).

A similarity of ideas makes it possible for us to refer here to other texts which may or may not be Pauline. In the Epistle to the Hebrews (5:5-6; cf. 1:3), this quality of the Son of God is interpreted in terms of high-priesthood. The Letter to the Ephesians (1:19ff.) exalts the power that God has put into operation in Christ by raising him from the dead to sit at his right hand in heaven. What is particularly interesting, however, is that this epistle goes on from this theme to consider a list of charisms: 'He who descended is he (*autos estin*) who also ascended far above all the heavens, that he might fill all things. And his gifts were that some should be apostles, some prophets, some evangelists, some pastors and teachers ... ' (4:10-11). Clearly, as in 1 Cor 12 and Rom 12, all this is for the purpose of building up the Body of Christ, which is a task to be shared by all the 'saints' (4:12). The gifts that build up the Church, then, come from the glorified Lord, 'from whom the whole body, joined and knit together by every joint with which it is supplied, when each part is working properly, makes bodily growth and upbuilds itself in love' (4:16).

It is a mistake to think, as I did in 1953 [in *The Mystery of the Church*] that a kind of 'free sector' reserved for the Holy Spirit exists alongside the operation of the instituted structures and means of grace.[37] The whole of Christian history bears witness to the fact that this freedom really exists, but it is the freedom of the living and glorified Lord Jesus together with his Spirit. They are what Irenaeus called in a very fine image the 'two hands of God'.[38]

In the Middle Ages a different image was used, that of the head and the heart in a living body. Who was the head and who was the heart? Was it Christ or the Spirit? The great theologians of the thirteenth century, Albert, Bonaventure and Thomas, referred to the *De motu cordis* of Aristotle, for whom the heart was the principle of life, on the basis of which a man was constructed and lived.[39] Bonaventure arrived at the idea that Christ was the heart of the Church and so expressed his own fervent Christocentrism. Christ is for him the *medius*, the middle,[40] and the sovereign *hierarcha* of the world, giving the Holy Spirit and all the *charismata*.[41] Thomas Aquinas, on the other hand, relying on Aristotle and his Arabic commentators, makes the Holy Spirit the heart of the Church.[42] He develops a very substantial theology of Christ as the Head of the Church. His objection and his reply to the question *Utrum Christus sit caput Ecclesiae*, 'Whether Christ is the Head of the Church' are as follows:[43]

Objection 3: In man, the head is a special member which receives a (vital) inflow from the heart. Christ is a universal principle for the Church. He is therefore not its head.
Reply: The head is in a position of obvious eminence with regard to the other external members, but the heart exercises a (vital) hidden inflow. That is why it is identified with the Holy Spirit, who gives life to and unites the Church in an invisible manner. As for the head, Christ is identified with it according to the visible nature according to which a man is placed above others.

Every movement is controlled by the head, and by 'movement' Thomas means all change, every transition of the 'flesh' towards union with God through grace. Christ, however, receives all the grace from which he himself lives and which he communicates to others from the Holy Spirit. That is why, Thomas teaches, the grace that Christ communicates to his Body, the Church, is the same as that with which he is himself filled in a sovereign manner. It is also why the same Holy Spirit, who makes Christ holy, is also in his Body, that is, in us, *unus numero in Christo et in omnibus*, 'one both in Christ and in all men'.[44] Thomas therefore often says that the Holy Spirit, who is identically the same, is the final complement of the unity of the Church. On one occasion at least he speaks of the 'Church of the Holy Spirit'.[45] This is, however, the Body of Christ. Thomas distinguishes the two by saying that the author of grace is God alone, Christ in his divinity or the Holy Spirit, but Christ is the instrument of its communication, not an inert or mechanical instrument, but one that is intelligent, free and joined as an organ, in such a way that he acts through the Holy Spirit or that the Holy Spirit acts through him. *Et ideo quidquid fit per Spiritum Sanctum etiam fit per Christum* — 'And therefore whatever is done by the Holy Spirit is also done by Christ'.[46]

It is possible to conclude from this impressive theological teaching that the Spirit is a reserve of impersonal energy and that the directives and decisions come from Christ, who is the head and the brain. Once again, however, this theology presupposes a pneumatological Christology, to which I shall return. The Spirit is the Spirit of the Word, of the Lord, of the Son, of Christ. Thomas stresses this again and again. But Jesus Christ is also of the Spirit, not only in his conception, but also in his messianic activity and in his being raised to the quality of 'Lord'. It is primarily in Christ that the 'two hands' of the Father, the Word and the Breath, are united.

Prophecy

Paul gives a high priority to 'prophecy' in his list of charisms, placing it second after that of being an apostle. Up until recently, the Church has claimed the active presence of this charism within itself, in a way that we shall have to consider later. 'The church cannot exist without bishops and priests, whatever their human qualities, but inwardly it lives and breathes through saints, apostles and prophets, religious geniuses, artists, heroes and ascetics'.[47] What, then, is prophecy? And what constitutes a prophet?

The phenomenon of prophecy existed outside Israel, but biblical prophetism, which was a striking feature in the life of the people of Israel for almost a millennium, is characterized by a truly unique homogeneity, power and purity.[48] The prophets of Israel spoke in the name of a God who was the living God and in the name of the unconditional nature of his rule, his plan and his demands. I shall concern myself here, however, above all with prophetism in the New Testament and in the history of the Church.

Luke refers several times to prophets in the Acts of the Apostles. Prophets came from Jerusalem to Antioch (11:27; see also 15:32; 21:10, where the prophet mentioned comes from Judaea). Their prophecy could take the form of a prediction of the future (11:28; 21:11; cf. 20:23). But Luke also speaks, as Paul will, of 'prophesying', not necessarily by those with the title of 'prophet' (19:6; 2:9, Philip's four unmarried daughters[49]). He also gives the title of prophet to men such as Barnabas (13:1), whom he also describes as an 'apostle' together with Paul (in the wider sense of the term: 14:4, 14). Barnabas had also received the gifts of *paraklēsis* or 'consolation' (4:36), discernment (9:27; 11:22-25) and strengthening or encouraging his brethren (11:23).

Paul's manner of speaking about prophecy is the most relevant for us today. Although he always treats it as a charism, he speaks about it in two ways. Sometimes he sees it simply as an activity. In such cases, in which women can be involved, he uses the verb. At other times, when he is speaking of a state in the Church, namely that of the prophet, the word is not found in the feminine. Chapter 14 of 1 Corinthians throws considerable light on what a Christian assembly at Corinth might have been — but see also 1:11-13 and 11:17-22! God intervenes and believers receive their gifts from him. The great rule is that the purpose of these gifts is to edify and to be useful to others and to the community as such. Paul uses three words: edify, exhort (*paraklēsis*) and encourage. Prophecy is only exceptionally a prediction of the future in Paul's letters and, when he speaks of it in this way, it only means a disclosure of God's intention about a life.[50] Thus, it would seem, the prophecies pronounced over Timothy (1 Tim 1:18; 4:14; cf. Acts 13:1-3) indicated his vocation, which was consecrated by his ordination. The one who prophesies expresses what God wants to communicate. This may be something mysterious (see 1 Cor 13:2), it may be almost commonplace, a simple word of encouragement.

C. Perrot has expressed very well what St Paul means when he refers to those who have the title of 'prophets'[51] and I will quote from this article at length.

Among the people who prophesy, some believers are distinguished from others to such a degree that they constitute a class of prophets. Examples of this are 1 Cor 14:29: 'Let two or three prophets speak' and 14:32: 'The spirits of prophets are subject to prophets'. The question is beyond dispute in 1 Cor 12:28: 'God has appointed in the church first apostles, second prophets, third teachers' (cf. Rom 12:6 and Eph 4:11). Here Paul is not simply speaking about parts to be played under the inflow of the Spirit, based on the model of the charisms that follow (the gift of miracles, speaking in tongues). He is pointing to persons or rather classes of persons, in hierarchical order, with a certain function to fulfil. Unlike Luke, Paul does not give any names, and so no personal identification is possible. The title of prophet seems to be attached not to an individual as such, but to the order within which the individual who prophesies is situated, according to the degree of his own charism: 'one by one' (1 Cor 14:31).

In other words, 'prophet' is clearly a 'corporate' rather than an individual professional title. What is more, according to Paul, such a group is not strictly established by the Church, but simply recognized by it. At the level of the individual, each one has to know whether he 'thinks that he is a prophet, or spiritual' (1 Cor 14:37). The individual, however, is always dependent on the Church's judgement. The other prophets and the whole community have to discern the true from the false prophet (1 Cor 14:29; 1 Thess 5:21: 'test everything')...

Both in the Pauline writings and in Acts, then, the Christian prophet is a charismatic who is integrated into a particular group within the Church. He has a function that operates both occasionally, under the inflow of God's unique grace, and permanently, through the individual's integration into the group of prophets. At this level, the opposition that certain modern theologians have stressed between so-called 'charismatic' and 'institutional' ministries is clearly artificial. All the ministries are charismatic and there is no group of ministries that is not institutional. St Paul himself was the first to outline the modalities by which the charismatic group of prophets carried out their task institutionally (see 1 Cor 14:39-40: '... all things should be done decently and in order'). There is no sign here of the prophet as an isolated figure who is able to make his title of prophet felt outside the function that he exercises within the community and the group to which he is attached and which ultimately judges him.

I have already pointed out that prophets are always named in the second place after 'apostles' in the Epistles that are indisputably Pauline. In Ephesians, however, a different and, in my opinion, important question is presented. In 2:20, believers are said to be 'built upon the foundation of the apostles and prophets' and, in 3:5, we are told that the mystery of Christ 'was not made known to the sons of men in other generations as it has now been revealed to his holy apostles and prophets by the Spirit'. In both cases, the two words are closely connected — the article is not repeated. This is one reason why E. Cothenet, who mentions other examples, has maintained that these 'apostles and prophets' are the same persons; they are apostles who are prophets. There is only one foundation laid on the foundation stone, Christ, and that is the foundation of the apostles who are regarded here as prophets.

Following the opinion of most exegetes, I believe that these are prophets of the Church, not prophets of the old dispensation. But is it necessary to identify them with the apostles? Many authors believe that they are charismatics of the Church. It is not essential to think of the 'foundation' in an exclusively historical or chronological way. It is something that is still present here and now. Does the function that Cothenet quite rightly recognizes as having been carried out by the New Testament prophets generally and those mentioned in Eph 4:11 in particular[52] not form part of that foundation?

In my view, what we have here is an inspired explanation of Scripture, in other words, the apostolic testimony providing us with our only knowledge of Jesus Christ. It is an assimilation by the Church of what was affirmed at the beginning once and for all time by the apostles (and it is to be noted that only four out of the nine New Testament authors are apostles). It is, at the level of a 'foundation' that is not exclusively chronological, a ministry of living faithfulness to the original testimony and kerygma.[53] There is no discontinuity between the one who plants, Paul, and the one who waters, Apollos, because God is the one who gives growth (1 Cor 3:4ff.). In the same way, there is also no discontinuity between the one who lays the foundation and the one who builds on it (1 Cor 3:10). The guarantee and criterion of continuity is the one foundation, Christ and his gospel. That continuity is guided by the Holy Spirit, but always with reference to Christ (note the equivalence in Eph 2:21, 22 of 'in the Lord' and 'in the Spirit'). In these conditions, there is co-operation between the Holy Spirit and Christ in the work of building up the Church of God. I would add to this what the fourth gospel says about the part played by the Paraclete: 'He will not speak on his own authority, but whatever he hears he will speak and he will declare to you all the things that are to come' (16:13). This interpretation has the advantage of establishing a continuity between the constitutive period of revelation and the time of the Church. This can be well illustrated by the vision of Karl Rahner.

There is a close link between what has already been said (by Christ) and what has not yet been said. At the conclusion of his article in *Lumière et Vie* from which I have quoted above, C. Perrot asked the following question: 'Is the prophetic office still at work nowadays?' His reply was: 'Yes and no'. His affirmative answer can be extended and illustrated by the following question and answer given by the editorial board at the end of the same number of the journal under the heading: 'Some Questions':

What does Christian prophetism mean nowadays? It is, we may say, a prophetism centred on Jesus himself. But what does that mean? How and in what respect is prophecy centred on Jesus?

No one would disagree that it is not enough to say that the name of Jesus should be pronounced. As for his Spirit, Jesus himself has told us that 'he blows where he will'. If we really believe that the Spirit of Jesus blows where he will, we cannot simply be satisfied with discerning that Spirit on the basis of what we already know about Jesus from the Scriptures and the traditions of the churches.

It is rather where the Spirit blows that there may be prophetic words spoken in the name of Jesus. If that is the case, how can prophecy simply come from the community of believers? Is it not also addressed to that community from outside itself? In that sense, faith and prophecy certainly cannot have the same status. Faith in Jesus can only be explicit. Can the same be said about prophetism? Is there not a prophetism according to the Spirit of Christ, which may lack any explicit reference to Jesus? In the end, should we not admit that there is nowadays a form of prophetism which has passed over into atheism, but which is no less prophesying in the Spirit of Jesus? In that sense, the assembly of believers should, in the name of their faith in a Spirit who blows where he will, recognize that prophecy does not belong exclusively to them any longer and that Jesus' words come to them nowadays by ways that they cannot prepare or discern in advance.[54]

This is explicitated by a movement from orthodoxy to orthopraxis. It is not so much a question of listening to Jesus as of following him and continuing his struggle for mankind (see below, note 54).

We would, of course, expect to find the opposite expressed by Karl Barth, whose theology was so Christocentric and so marked by what Dietrich Bonhoeffer called his positivism of revelation. For instance:

> There is only one unique, irrevocable and unrepeatable revelation ... One single fact constitutes the Church as Church, namely that man listens because God has spoken and still speaks and that he listens to what God has told him and tells him again and again ... .[55]

> No man declares the will of God, except in terms of Christ, who is the only real prophet. The point is, therefore, that we must not fancy ourselves as private prophets; no; we do not need any new discoveries in the realm of the divine. All we need has been said and we have just to repeat it. To take part in the prophecy means for us to be pupils in the House of God.[56]

Yet, like Bonhoeffer, Barth is one of the great prophets of our own age! I am with both of them. This brings me to the question: Does the charism of prophecy still exist nowadays? Has it continued in the Church? Is it to be found outside its visible boundaries? My answer is certainly 'yes', but I would like to distinguish several different forms of prophetism, since the word has a very extended application. Purely for the sake of clarity, I shall number the concluding sections of this chapter.

(1) The early Church recognized that it possessed the charism of prophecy.[57] Leaving aside the *Didache*, in which prophets are certainly mentioned, because of the uncertainty about its date of composition and its true nature, we can begin with Polycarp, who was called an 'apostolic and prophetic teacher'.[58] Justin Martyr maintained that the prophetic charisms had passed from the Jews to Christians.[59] Irenaeus wrote in or about A.D. 180: 'We know that, in the Church, many brethren have prophetic charisms and speak by virtue of the Holy Spirit in various tongues... revealing the mysteries of God. They are what the Apostle calls "spiritual men" '.[60]

The Montanist movement did not lead to this conviction being abandoned and one of its opponents, Miltiades, wrote: 'The Apostle thinks that the prophetic charism is bound to exist in the whole of the Church until the last parousia'.[61] It did, however, tend to disappear after Montanism. Origen says that it was needed at the beginning of the Church's life, but that it ceased to be necessary later.[62] What was the precise meaning of these examples of prophetism? Were they merely cases of paraenesis — exhortation and encouragement? Were they ecstatic states? Or were they acts of prediction?

In the form or sense of discourse about the future, prophecy has often reappeared, especially at times of revolutionary social change or historical crisis.[63] The documentation compiled by von Döllinger well illustrates the link between it and a particular interpretation of history and very frequently a desire to support certain national, dynastic, popular, pontifical or spiritual claims. Buoyed up by fervour, in extreme cases by fanaticism, feeding on the expectations, hopes, militancy with a view to the future to be found in most men, imagination has constructed Utopias or given an outlet to fears, hatreds and partisanship. Hence those discourses on the Antichrist, the punishment or the destruction of Rome, or, on the other hand, the *Papa* or *Pastor Angelicus*, the Muslims and the Holy Land, the end of the world. The modern world abounds with echoes of such 'discourses'. From time to time, people talk again of the 'prophecy of Malachi' or Nostradamus; the 'third secret of Fatima' recruits its Blue Army. On the other hand, the real sanctity of St Vincent Ferrer, for instance, is not prejudiced by the inaccuracy of his predictions. Some people stand out from the mass of humanity because of their unique strength or importance. Consider Hildegard of Bingen, who had the approval of three Popes and numerous saints and for whom I still have a private devotion for personal reasons. Consider Joachim of Fiore, who at any rate encouraged a movement of creativity and aroused an expectation of a new future. Consider Savonarola, whose lively sense of the future was recognized by von Döllinger. Consider the historic role of so many enthusiasts, the important part played in this story by women: Hildegard, Elizabeth of Schönau, Bridget of Sweden, Catherine of Siena, Joan of Arc...

There have been many authentic prophets in our own times — men who have seen into the future: Félicité de Lammenais, whom Victor Hugo called 'terrifying with future', Charles Péguy ... And since John XXIII and Vatican II, we have been urged to understand the 'signs of the times'.

(2)   Following the meaning that I have given to the 'prophets' in Eph 2:20 and 3:5, it is possible to regard an understanding in depth of Scripture and the divine mysteries as an extension of early prophetism. This appears to have been the view of some Church Fathers.[64] It is also, in my opinion, what Newman meant by the 'prophetic tradition', which he distinguished from the episcopal tradition. He saw that tradition as the whole complex or chain of explanations, interpretations and expressions of faith provided by the doctors and spiritual writers of the Church and even found in the Church's liturgies and devotions.[65]

This is obviously connected with what I said at the end of the previous section and what I shall say in the next.

The current demand for prophets in the Church is due in part to the revolutionary changes in our time. Under pain of irrelevance the Church can no longer ignore the course of world history. The rapidly evolving secular culture of our day puts questions to the Church for which there are no ready-made solutions. Scrutinizing the signs of the times, Christianity must reinterpret its own doctrine and goals in relation to the world of today. To effect this transposition without loss of substance is a task calling for prophetic insight.[66]

Prophetic insight, clearly, in faithfulness to the Christological confession of faith of the apostles (1 Cor 12:3; 1 Jn 4:2) and in communion with the faith and the discernment of the Church (1 Thess 5:21; 1 Jn 4:1; Rom 12:6, where the *Traduction oecuménique* has 'in agreement with faith' [see NJB note here]).

(3)   If the prophetic gift in the widest sense of the term must subsist in the Church in order to keep it in the truth of God's revelation and the faith of the apostles, then the whole body will be prophetic. Vatican II was perhaps too timid in this respect, but it said this quite formally.[67] The Church is an organic, structured body in which all members are alive, but they do not do the same thing, nor do they do it in the same way. There are 'brethren' and there are pastors. The latter have their own charism, in accordance with their particular mission.

The words of Irenaeus are well known: *His qui in ecclesia sunt presbyteris oboedire oportet, his qui successionem habent ab apostolis, sicut ostendimus, qui cum episcopatus successione charisma veritatis certum secundum placitum Patris acceperunt*, 'We ought to obey those presbyters who are in the Church, who have their succession from the apostles, as we have shown, and who with their succession in the episcopate have received the sure charism of truth according to the Father's pleasure'.[68]

The precise meaning of the excellent phrase *charisma veritatis certum*, translated here as 'the sure charism of truth', is disputed and for this reason was included in the Dogmatic Constitution *Dei Verbum* (8, 2) without any reference to Irenaeus. Some scholars have understood it in the objective sense as the content and the burden of the Tradition received by the bishops with their succession and as the gift of truth itself.[69] Others have understood *charisma* here to mean a personal spiritual gift. This is not, however, a gift given for the function of bishop as such, but rather a gift which is recognized in that believer and by virtue of which he is called to be given the function of the episcopate.[70] There are at the same time valid reasons for regarding this phrase as an expression of an infallible — or at least indefectible — grace of teaching that is received with the succession at ordination. These reasons are based above all on the context of the text, but they are also supported by liturgical, biblical and other patristic references.[71]

Charles Journet believed that 'prophetic knowledge [is] not extinct in the Church' and that it is to be found in the Church's *magisterium*. In this context, he also made a number of very rigorous distinctions,[72] which can be summarized as follows. There is in the first place prophecy in the strict sense of the word as a grace of revelation; this was the privilege of the apostles. After them, there is prophecy as a contemplative and spiritual understanding of the truth, and there are also, possibly, revelations which have practical actions in view. Finally, there is the grace that is specifically related to the presence of the *magisterium* that is guaranteed to the Catholic Church.

Journet was particularly critical of an extension of the content of revelation and the faith that is in accordance with it to include 'prophetism' in a very wide sense; he illustrated this by texts from Nicholas Berdyaev. It is a fact that attempts have often been made to justify very dubious initiatives of all kinds, most of them departing from the accepted norms, by an appeal to the excellent but vague category of 'prophetism', and the Catholic Church has not been the only one to react against this.[73]

In theory at least, the *magisterium* has become too isolated from the whole body of the Church. In fact, it can only be certain of its real hierarchical charism within a communion of faith and love with that body and in serving it. The argument that it is possible for a Pope to be a heretic, with the way it is traditionally explained, is an extreme case that is necessary for a proper theology of the *magisterium*, which does justice to the very profound truth contained in the Orthodox idea of *sobornost*, community.

If there is one sphere in which the Spirit's reference to the Word is affirmed, it is certainly the one just discussed. Popes, councils and theologians have vied with each other throughout the history of the Church in proclaiming that the Holy Spirit is present in the Church and the Church's *magisterium* purely for the purpose of maintaining faithfully and, if necessary, defining what is contained or implied in the Word of God or revelation.

(4)   It should be noted that 'prophesying' of the kind outlined in chapter 14 of 1 Corinthians is practised in meetings of the (charismatic) Renewal. It consists of spontaneous words of encouragement, edification and exhortation and possibly even of throwing light on divine mysteries; more rarely, a precise indication about the future, an action to be taken, a decision in life. As in 1 Cor 12:10 and 14:29, there is a place here for discernment, which has its own rules of health.

(5)   The terms 'prophet', 'prophetic' and 'prophetism' have become widely used and distinctly favoured in recent years.[74] They have been employed above all to describe a certain type of man (less frequently, woman) and a certain kind of commitment. Some names can be cited: Martin Luther King, Teilhard de Chardin, Cardinal Cardijn, Vincent Lebbe, Pope John XXIII, Helder Câmara, Solzhenitsyn, Dietrich Bonhoeffer and Mgr Riobé. These are all men who abandoned the *status quo* and pointed ways towards the future. They perceived something and were seized by their vision. They may have encountered apathy and opposition, but they opened up a path for something that was aspiring to life. Their task in the Church and the world was to reveal to others the end of God's plan for his kingdom, to which the biblical idea of truth I have discussed above corresponds. The Spirit is the Spirit of truth. From the very beginning, he has also been called the one 'who has spoken through the prophets'. The same Spirit awakened in them a call and an intense conviction that made them 'born again'; their experience of rebirth led them to their commitment.

I have so far considered principally 'religious' prophets. In the Church, they have been founders of orders and reforming movements. Nowadays, however, we are above all concerned with man himself. We have also experienced revolutions and movements of liberation like the wartime French Resistance. We prefer non-conformists. We admire those who reject and denounce the *status quo* that favours only those who are secure and firmly established. Such prophets are above all workers for liberation, committed to the poor and against oppression and racism. The prophets of the Old Testament are cited rather than those of the New, and the praxis of 'Jesus of Nazareth' rather than the Christ of St Paul. The point of reference is the kingdom of God, the object of hope, rather than the dogma of the Church. Many would certainly recognize themselves in these words of Georges Bernanos: 'I am an obedient son of the Church, but I am also in impatient communion with all those in revolt, all the disappointed, all the unheard, all the damned in this world'.

We have heard from Vatican II, Medellín, Paul VI, the 1971 Synod of Bishops, John Paul II and Archbishop Romero that liberation is an essential part of evangelization. This movement has its martyrs, and they fully deserve this title.[75] It also has its prophets.

Opposition to these prophets and rejection of their message clearly derives from conservatism, but conservatism can have varying motives. One is attachment to the *status quo*. Young Protestants once appeared at a church assembly with banners proclaiming: 'We are the mothballs of the world!' Another reason is dogmatic certainty — we already know and have all the answers, and so we do not listen to the questions. The Word — misunderstood, no doubt — is an obstacle to the Breath. We do not, after all, know where the Breath comes from or where it is going!

In 1980, on the eve of Pentecost, I was interviewed on Swiss television and expounded my idea of the Word and the Breath. My interviewer then asked me: 'Are there, in your opinion, two churches — the established Church and the Church of the future?' A few days later, I read an article by Henri Fesquet in *Le Monde* of 25-26 May entitled 'Pentecost, the feast of the Holy Spirit. God in the Future'. But there is only one liturgical cycle and it is centred on Christ. Pentecost is the fiftieth day of the feast of the Easter season. It is true that it involves the future of Christ, what Tennyson called 'the Christ that is to be'. It initiates 'Christ in the future', but that Christ is still Christ. The Spirit displays something that is new, in the novelty of history and the variety of cultures, but it is a new thing that comes from the fullness that has been given once for all by God in Christ.

That fullness has not been totally revealed or totally fulfilled in Christ according to the flesh. For it to be fulfilled, it had to be filled with the Spirit, and for it to be revealed, the Spirit had to dwell in the apostles and prophets; Paul, the supernumerary apostle, had to be called by Christ in glory; and the 'mystery' had to be revealed to the 'saints' (Col 1:26; Eph 3:3-5). This 'mystery' that is expounded at the beginning of the Epistle to the Ephesians is that of the economy of grace that is unfolded in history. For this to happen, John, the last of the Twelve to survive, had to be the theologian both of the incarnate Word, who reveals the Father, *and* of the Paraclete.

Paul (in 1 Cor 12:3) and John (in 1 Jn 4:2) make the testimony borne to the Lord Jesus a criterion of the activity of the Spirit. He brings something new into the course of history, but that novelty is not something vague and imprecise. In Luther's magnificent term, the Spirit is not a 'sceptic'.[76] The Word may be permeated with the Spirit, but the Spirit is also permeated with the Word. The two are inseparable. They both proceed from the Father.

There is only one Church of God, which is at once the established Church and the Church of the future, and is built up by the 'two hands' of God! Those two hands are also what God uses to make men one with himself. This places us firmly in the profound theology of the 'divine missions' and the continuity between the economic and the immanent Trinity that I expounded in *I Believe in the Holy Spirit*.

Notes

1 References and a bibliography will be found in my *L'Eglise de S. Augustin à l'époque moderne* (*Histoire des dogmes*, III, 3; Paris, 1970), pp. 198-209. R. A. Knox attempted to write such a history, but his *Enthusiasm. A Chapter in the History of Religion* (Oxford, 1950), is frequently disappointing, although parts of it are interesting.

2 I have derived considerable help in what follows from C. Ehlinger (ed.), *Guide illustré de l'histoire du christianisme* (Paris, 1983).

3 J. Edwards, *Faithful Narrative of the Surprising Works of God* (1735).

4 Clive Dillon-Malone specializes in this question. A summary of the conclusions drawn from his studies will be found in 'New Religions in Africa', *Concilium* 161 (1983), 55-60.

5 I have relied here on Michel Guéry, *Christianisme céleste. Notes de travail. L'Eglise, la vie spirituelle*, published in 148 pages of duplicated text (3rd term, 1973).

6 Dorothy Sayers sought to give the other six their rightful place in her book *The Other Six Deadly Sins* (London, 1943).

7 Mansi 32, 1052.

8 Maurice Blondel, writing under the pseudonym 'Testis' and the surprising title 'La Semaine sociale de Bordeaux et le Monophorisme', *APhC* (1910).

9 See M. J. Scheeben, *Mysterien des Christentums* (1865), §80; *Dogmatik*, §7, 57; §8, 69 and 72; §10, 126; §22, 317; §23, 335ff.; §32, 502.

10 Georges Bernanos, *Le chemin de la croix des âmes* (Paris, 1948), p. 463. Other texts will be found in Hans Urs von Balthasar, *Le chrétien Bernanos* (Paris, 1956), pp. 73ff., 540ff.

11 *The Private Journal of Henri Frédéric Amiel* (New York, 1935), p. 70.

12 *Lamentabili* 21: *DS* 3421. This question became rather relevant to theologians when the Assumption of the Virgin Mary was proclaimed as a revealed dogma. See, for example, R. Spiazzi, 'Rivelazione compiuta con la morte degli Apostoli', *Greg* 33 (1952), 24-57; F. Malmberg, 'De afsluiting van het "depositum fidei" ', *Bijdr.* 13 (1952), 31-44. Since then, A. Michel, 'L'enseignement du Magistère et l'époque où fut close la Révélation', *Div.* V (1961), 849-864; J. Schumacher, cited below (note 29).

13 See A. Loisy, *Autour d'un petit livre* (1903), pp. 196ff., 207; article in *RMM* (1931), 531-533; *Mémoires* III (1931), p. 339; *Simples réflexions sur le décret du Saint Office 'Lamentabili'* (1908), pp. 58, 139.

14 See Tyrrell's reply to Father Lebreton in *RAp* IV (1907, 2), 508ff., 519; *Suis-je catholique?* (1909), pp. 23-24, 151, 171-194, 217-218.

15 George Tyrrell, *Through Scylla and Charybdis* (1907), p. 324.

16 A. Loisy, *RHLR* (1911), 609. See also L. da Veiga Coutinho, *Tradition et histoire dans la Controverse moderniste (1898-1910)* (Rome, 1954), p. 61.

17 H. de Lubac, *La postérité spirituelle de Joachim de Flore*, I: *De Joachim à Schelling*, II: *De Saint-Simon à nos jours* (Paris, 1979, 1981).

18 Jacob Böhme, *Mysterium Magnum*: 'The Spirit of Christ in his children is not bound to any special form, according to which he may say nothing that is not found in the apostolic letters. Just as the Spirit was free in the Apostles, so too does the Spirit of Christ still speak through the mouth of his children and he does not need any formula prepared in advance and derived from a literal formula'. Cited by de Lubac, *op. cit.*, I, p. 220.

19 H. de Lubac, *op. cit.*, I, p. 283.

20 Yves Congar, *Tradition and Traditions* (London, 1966), pp. 120-137.

21 Texts *ibid.*, pp. 107-118. See also J. Beumer, 'Das katholische Schriftprinzip in der theologischen Literatur der Scholastik bis zur Reformation', *Schol.* 16 (1941), 24-52; B. Decker, ' "Sola Scriptura" bei Thomas von Aquin', *Festschrift für Bischof A. Stohr* (Mainz, 1960), pp. 117-129; B. Tierney, ' "Sola Scriptura" and the Canonists', *Studia Gratiana* XI (1967), pp. 347-366; H. Schlüsser, *Der Primat der Heiligen Schrift als theologisches und kanonistisches Problem im Spätmittelalter* (Wiesbaden, 1977). And of course see the four volumes of H. de Lubac, *L'Exégèse médiévale* (Paris 1959-64).

22 H. de Lubac, 'Le problème du développement du dogme', *RSR* 35 (1948), 130-160.

23 K. Rahner, 'The Development of Dogma', *Theological Investigations* 1 (London and Baltimore, 1961), pp. 39-77.

24 E. Schillebeeckx, *Revelation and Theology* (London and Melbourne, 1967), pp. 13-15, 28 note 1, 66ff.

25 See H. de Lubac's commentary, *Vatican II. La Révélation divine* II (*Unam Sanctam* 70a; Paris, 1968), pp. 215-240. For a rejection of the formula, see p. 252.

26 Y. Congar, 'La crédibilité des révélations privées', art. first pub. 1937, repr. in *Sainte Eglise* (*Unam Sanctam* 41; Paris, 1963), pp. 375-392. Karl Rahner, *Visionen und Prophezeiungen* (Freiburg, 1958) stresses the fact that private revelations concern the whole Church and sometimes contribute something new to its life.

27 See D.-M. Abbrescia, *Elena Guerra (1835-1914), Profetismo e rinnovamento* (Brescia, n.d. [= 1982]).

28 See L. Cerfaux, 'Pour l'histoire du titre Apostolos dans le Nouveau Testament', *RSR* 46 (1960), 76-92.

29 This is the thesis of Karl Rahner, *Über die Schriftinspiration* (*Quaestiones disputatae*; Innsbruck, 1960) and J. Schumacher, *Der apostolische Abschluss der Offenbarung Gottes* (Freiburg, 1979). I would not criticize Rahner now in exactly the same way as I criticized him in *RSPhTh* 45 (1961), 32-42.

30 R. Sohm, *Kirchenrecht* I (1892). See my study, 'Rudolf Sohm nous interroge encore', *RSPhTh* 57 (1973), 263-294.

31 H. von Campenhausen, *Kirchliches Amt und geistliche Vollmacht in den ersten drei Jahrhunderten* (Tübingen, 1953). Von Campenhausen does not, like Sohm, oppose charism and law in principle. He is conscious only of a difference between the earliest Pauline communities which lived on the basis of free charisms and in which the leaders had no hierarchical position, and the Judaean communities with their instituted elders. The communities with a charismatic basis, however, developed legal structures in order to survive.

32 U. Brockhaus, *Charisma und Amt. Die paulinische Charismenlehre auf dem Hintergrund der frühchristlichen Gemeindefunktionen* (Wuppertal, 1972).

33 See 1 Thess 5:12 (*proïstamenoi*); Heb 13:17 (*hēgoumenoi*); 1 Cor 16:15-16; cf. 12:28 (*kubernēsis*); Phil 1:1 (*episkopoi, diakonoi*).

34 Brockhaus defines Paul's sense of paraenesis (*op. cit.*, p. 146), as 'guidance given for the life of the individual Christian or the community of believers, based on the salvation given in Christ and orientated towards the Lord who is to come again and towards the ultimate consummation'.

35 H. Schlier, 'L'objet principal de la première épître aux Corinthiens', *Le temps de l'Eglise* (1961), p. 160. The German text first appeared in 1948.

36 See my *I Believe in the Holy Spirit* I (London and New York, 1983), pp. 35-39.

37 See my first 'retraction' in *I Believe in the Holy Spirit, op. cit.*, II, pp. 11-12.

38 *Ibid.*, p. 9.

39 *Secundum autem Philosophi sententiam, prima pars est cor, quia a corde omnes virtutes animae per corpus diffundantur,* 'According to the opinion of the Philosopher, the principal part is the heart, because it is from the heart that all the virtues of the soul are spread throughout the body': Thomas Aquinas, *Comm. in Met.* V, 1 (ed. M. R. Cathala, 755).

40 See R. Šilič, *Christus und die Kirche. Ihr Verhältnis nach der Lehre des hl. Bonaventura* (*BSHT,* NS III; Breslau, 1938), pp. 53-74, especially according to the most complete text of Bonaventure, *Collationes in Hexaemeron,* ed. P. Delorme (Rome, 1934), Coll. 1, nos 19-20.

41 R. Šilič, *op. cit.*, pp. 138-141. Bonaventure seldom uses the title of Christ the Head, preferring that of *hierarcha*: see pp. 44 note 141 and 69 note 52.

42 See M. Grabmann, *Die Lehre des hl. Thomas von Aquin von der Kirche als Gotteswerk* (Regensburg, 1903), pp. 184-193.

43 Thomas Aquinas *ST* IIIa q. 8, a. 1, ad 3. See also *De Ver.* q. 29 , a. 4, ad 7.

44 *Idem, In III Sent.* d. 13, q. 2, a. 1, ad 2; *De Ver.* q. 29, a. 4; *Comm. in ev. Ioan,* c. 1, lect. 9 and 10; *ST* IIa IIae, q. 183, a. 3, ad 3. The idea was taken up again by Pius XII in his encyclical *Mystici Corporis,* 54 and 77 *ad sensum:* see *AAS* 35 (1943), 219 and 230: and by Vatican II in the Dogmatic Constitution *Lumen Gentium* 7, 7.

45 Thomas Aquinas, *Comm. in ev. Matt.* c. 20, lect. 6.

46 *Idem, Comm. in Eph.* c. 1, lect. 5. See also *Comm. in Rom.* c. 12, lect. 2; *ST* IIIa, q. 8, a. 1; Ia, q. 32, a. 1, ad 3: *Salus generis humani quae perficitur per Filium incarnatum et per donum Spiritus Sancti,* 'The salvation of mankind which is

accomplished by the incarnate Son and by the gift of the Holy Spirit'.

47 N. Berdyaev, *The Destiny of Man* (London, 1937), p. 105.

48 'Prophètes', *DBS* VIII (1969-72), gives firstly (cols 692-811) articles on each of the Old Testament prophets before the letter P [and not already published in *DBS*]; secondly (cols 812-908) a study of prophetism in the East, outside Israel; thirdly (cols 909-1222) an extensive study of biblical (Old Testament) prophetism by L. Ramlot; and fourthly (cols 1222-1337) a detailed study of the theme in the New Testament by E. Cothenet. See also '*prophētēs*', *TDNT* VI, pp. 781-786, by H. Krämer, R. Rendtorff, R. Meyer and G. Friedrich, the author of the section concerned with the New Testament (pp. 829-861). In the German edition, the Tables, *ThWNT* X, 2 (1979), pp. 1250-1254, include a very full bibliography of publications from 1957 onwards. See also C. Perrot, 'Prophètes et prophétisme dans le Nouveau Testament', *LV* (November-December 1973), 25-39. There are also the texts of a colloquium held at the Ecumenical Institute at Bossey: J. Panagopoulos (ed.), *Prophetic Vocation in the New Testament and Today* (*NT.S* XLV; Leiden, 1977). Despite the 'Today' of the title, these specialized studies hardly take the contemporary situation into account, except for the World Council of Churches' Programme to Combat Racism.

49 Women are reported as prophesying in 1 Cor 11:5; 14:33-35; also in the Old Testament. See G. Friedrich, *op. cit.*, *TDNT*, VI, p. 829.

50 G. Friedrich, *ibid.*

51 C. Perrot, *op. cit.* (note 48), pp. 29, 30.

52 E. Cothenet, *op. cit.*, *DBS*, cols 1286, 1318; *idem*, 'Les prophètes chrétiens comme exégètes charismatiques de l'Ecriture', *Prophetic Vocation, op. cit.* (note 48). H. Greeven, 'Propheten, Lehrer, Vorsteher bei Paulus', *ZNW* 44 (1952-53), 28ff., and several of the authors contributing to *Prophetic Vocation*, have pointed out that there is neither a separation nor a clear distinction between prophets and teachers or doctors in the New Testament. Cothenet, however, *Prophetic Vocation, op. cit.*, p. 102, draws attention to certain differences: '*didachē* ['teaching'] is more systematic, whereas prophecy occurs only occasionally and is directed more towards action'. See also D. Hill, p. 126, and H. Kraft, pp. 162ff., in the same volume.

53 Cothenet's interpretation is the same as that of L. Cerfaux, J. Pfammater, J. Murphy O'Connor and others. The interpretation that I favour is that of I. Knabenbauer; P. Ewald; E. Fascher, *Prophētēs* (Giessen, 1927), pp. 122ff.; P. Ketter; H. Bacht, *Bib* (1951), 237; R. Schnackenburg, *Cath(M)* (1961), 115; J. Gnilka, *Epheserbrief* (1971), p. 157; H. Schlier, *Brief an die Epheser* (3rd ed., 1962), p. 142; F. Schnider and W. Stenger, 'The Church as a Building and the Building up of the Church', *Concilium* 80 (10.8; December 1972), 28-32; P. Bony, *Le ministère et les ministères selon le Nouveau Testament* (1974), pp. 75-79; and finally J. Panagopoulos, *Prophetic Vocation, op. cit.*, pp. 17ff. Several of these references are cited at second hand.

54 C. Perrot, *LV* 115 (November-December 1973), 90-91. The text continues: 'Is the word not a prophetic word centred on Jesus whenever it urges men at a particular time and in a particular place to live in the same way as Jesus of

Nazareth lived? "In the same way" means: Not according to the letter, but by inaugurating for today a mode of existence that corresponds effectively to what Jesus' mode of existence was in his own times. Jesus did not, after all, live his life as a man for himself — he lived it for us. To such an extent, Paul tells us, that if we are not raised from the dead, Christ himself has not risen! Is not every word prophetic, then, simply because it has taken up a position in favour of a particular mode of human existence which makes the way in which Jesus lived present for men today? That would be achieved by taking up a position in favour of that way of being human that would proclaim the very meaning of Jesus' mode of existence'.

55 Karl Barth, *Révélation, Eglise, Théologie* (Paris, 1934), pp. 13 and 27.
56 *Idem, The Faith of the Church* (New York, 1958; London and Glasgow, 1960), p. 59.
57 Documentation will be found in G. Bardy, *La théologie de l'Eglise, de saint Clément de Rome à saint Irénée* (*Unam Sanctam* 13; Paris, 1945). See also E. Cothenet, *op. cit., DBS*, cols 1322-1324.
58 *Mart. Polycarpi* XVI, 2. This took place in A.D. 135.
59 Justin Martyr, *Dial.* LXXXII, 1; see also XXXIX, 2.
60 Irenaeus, *Adv. haer.* V, 6, 1; see also II, 32, 4. These texts are cited by Eusebius, *Hist. Eccl.* V, 7, 1-6.
61 Eusebius, *Hist. Eccl.* V, 17, 4. See also G. Bardy, *op. cit.*, p. 151.
62 Origen, *Contra Cels.* VII, 11 (*PG* 11, 1456-57).
63 See I. von Döllinger, *Der Weissagungsglaube und das Prophetentum in der christlichen Zeit* (1871); P. Alphandéry, 'Prophètes et ministère prophétique dans le moyen âge latin', *RHPhR* 12 (1932), 334-359; P. Boglioni, 'I carismi nella vita della Chiesa medioevale', *SacDot* (Bologna) 59 (1970), 383-430, especially 414ff.
64 Origen, *Comm. Ser.* 47 in *Matt.* (*PG* 13, 1669A): *Qui ecclesiastice docent verbum prophetae sunt Christi*, 'Those who teach the word in the Church are prophets of Christ'. See also Cyril of Alexandria, *In 1 Cor* 14:2 (*PG* 74, 889), cited by Cothenet: prophesying is simply interpreting the words of the prophets.
65 J. H. Newman, *Essays* I: *Apostolic Tradition* (July 1836), pp. 125ff.; *idem, The Prophetical Office in the Church* (1837), p. 112, reproduced, with notes and a valuable preface, in the third edition of the *Via Media*. See also J. Guitton, *La Philosophie de Newman. Essai sur l'idée de développement* (Paris, 1933), pp. 47-48.
66 A. Dulles, 'The Succession of Prophets in the Church', *Concilium* 34 (4.4; 1968), 28-32; quotation on 31.
67 Dogmatic Constitution *Lumen Gentium* 12, 35.
68 Irenaeus, *Adv. haer.* IV, 26, 2 (*PG* 7, 1053; ed. W. W. Harvey, II, 236).
69 See K. Müller, *ZNW* 23 (1924), 216-222; D. van den Eynde, *Les Normes de l'enseignement chrétien dans la littérature patristique des trois premiers siècles* (Gembloux and Paris, 1933), pp. 186-187; H. von Campenhausen, *op. cit.* (note 31); P. Bacq, *De l'ancienne à la nouvelle alliance selon S. Irénée. Unité du livre IV de l'Adv. haer.* (Paris, 1978), p. 202 note 2; H. Vogt, *ThQS* (1983), 225.
70 See E. Flesseman van Leer, *Tradition and Scripture in the Early Church* (Assen, 1954), pp. 119-122; R. P. C. Hanson, *Tradition in the Early Church* (London, 1962), pp. 159ff.

71 This has been the position of Protestant historians of dogma such as Harnack, Loofs, Sohm and Seeberg, who have regarded Irenaeus as the first to bear witness to the idea of hierarchy. For K. Müller, on the other hand, Hippolytus was the first. A better study is that of L. Ligier, 'Le *charisma veritatis certum* des évêques. Ses attaches liturgiques, patristiques et bibliques', *L'homme devant Dieu. Mélanges H. de Lubac* (Paris, 1964), I, pp. 247-268.

72 C. Journet, *The Church of the Word Incarnate*, I: *The Apostolic Hierarchy* (London and New York, 1955), pp. 132-141.

73 As Marc Boegner pointed out at the Faith and Order Conference at Edinburgh in 1937, 'It is dangerous to allow lay people to practise prophetism. This has been proved in the history of our Church, which has at times been disturbed by waves of prophetism. I want to encourage activity on the part of lay people, but not in prophecy'. This statement had the approval of Professor Hamilcar Alivisatos. See L. Hodgson (ed.), *The Second World Conference on Faith and Order* (London, 1938), pp. 161 and 162; cited by H. R. Weber in *Prophetic Vocation, op. cit.* (note 48), p. 220.

74 Hence, in my *Vraie et fausse réforme dans l'Eglise* (Paris, 1950), the chapter 'Prophètes et réformateurs', pp. 196-228; 2nd ed. (1969), pp. 175-207. See also *Concilium* 37 (7. 4; September 1968) and *LV* 115 (November-December 1973). R. de Haes' study, *Pour une théologie du prophétique. Lecture thématique de la théologie de Karl Rahner* (*Recherches Africaines de Théologie* 4; Louvain and Paris, 1972) is at a different level from my own. I would, however, mention Karl Rahner, *The Dynamic Element in the Church* (Freiburg and New York, 1964), the German original of which was published in 1958.

75 See *Concilium* 163 (*Martyrdom Today*; March 1983).

76 Luther, *De servo arbitrio* (1525; *WA* 18, 605, 31-34): *Spiritus sanctus non est Scepticus, nec dubia aut opiniones in cordibus nostris scripsit, sed assertiones ipsa vita et omni experientia certiores et firmiores*, 'The Holy Spirit is not a sceptic, nor has he written doubts or suppositions in our hearts, but declarations more certain and more firm than our own life and all experience'.

Appendix

The Spirit as co-instituting the Church
Are the charisms structuring principles of the Church?

The idea that institution and charism are opposed to each other can be abandoned. There is no shortage of good arguments to substantiate this conclusion.[1] There is, of course, a certain tension between the two — that is in the nature of things. We were, for example, often reminded of this 'tension' towards the end of the 1970s in the relationship between those theologians who were striving to achieve a renewal in a certain sphere and authority, especially that of Rome, in the Church. In this Appendix, I would like, along the general lines of this book, to complete what I said in the previous chapter by briefly discussing the two questions raised by the title above.

In the past, the Church was regarded in most Catholic teaching essentially as an unequal or hierarchical society, and attempts were made by Catholic apologists to prove that this was how Christ had founded the Church and how he wanted it to be. This claim was constantly disputed, especially by German Protestant critics. During the 1930s, however, more and more scholars came to agree with the idea that had already been put forward by a minority that Jesus' intention had been to bring together an original flock and that he had instituted the group of the Twelve.[2] Even if we go no further than the conclusions drawn from historical criticism, we can be quite certain that the pre-paschal Jesus had in view and foreshadowed the existence of a new People of God resulting from his proclamation of the kingdom of God and from the Twelve.[3]

There is, however, not a great gulf, but certainly a distance between what we learn from Paul's letters of twenty years after Jesus' death and the knowledge that we can gain of Jesus' intention with regard to the Church. And what are we to say if we read the Acts of the Apostles? Pentecost — not mentioned at all by Paul — appears in Acts as the beginning of a new creation. Jesus had left open a perspective of a new People or a kingdom on earth, lasting beyond his own life for an indeterminate time. In Acts, however, we are confronted with intense missionary activity and churches administering baptism, celebrating the Eucharist, professing faith and possessing ministers. In other words, what we call the Church results from the apostles and from Pentecost.

We should not, however, for this reason overlook the connection between this Pentecostal dimension and the work accomplished by Christ when he was in the flesh. This is, I think, what occurs to some extent, for example, in the attempt at systematization made by Leonardo Boff, when he says: 'Jesus did not preach the Church, but the kingdom of God' and 'The Church as an institution was not based, as is frequently claimed, on the Incarnation of the Word, but on faith in the power of the Apostles inspired by the Holy Spirit, who made them transfer eschatology to the time of the Church and teaching about the kingdom of God to teaching about the Church, an imperfect and temporal realization of the kingdom'.[4]

This insight has enabled Boff to see the Church as a reality that is open to forms or initiatives to which new circumstances might give rise. In these new situations, whether they exist now or in the future, the Church has to carry out its mission to 'make the risen Christ and his Spirit present in the world and to make his message of liberation, grace, forgiveness and boundless love heard' (p. 87). The new forms, may, Boff suggests, be the possibility for lay people, in view of the chronic shortage of ordained priests, to celebrate the Eucharist (pp. 90-100) or the possibility of ordaining women (pp. 101-140).

My reaction to these suggestions is not entirely negative. It is true that the Spirit of Pentecost has made the Church, through the apostles. It is true that the mission of the Church that is constantly enlivened by the same Spirit calls for new forms as required. We have, however, to preserve an equilibrium and that is, I think, threatened in this case.

The kingdom proclaimed by Jesus was not simply eschatological. As A.-L. Descamps has shown, it incorporated the vision that it would to some extent be accomplished here on earth after Jesus' death in a community resulting from him and the Twelve. The baptism and the Eucharist by which the churches were constituted came from the pre-paschal Jesus; so did the Twelve, and Jesus' words about the Father, the new form of justice, faith, and so on. The problem is always how to separate the work of the Word who reveals the Father from that of the Spirit. They co-institute the Church. The Spirit is not autonomous in the substantial aspect of the work to which the Word of God, the incarnate Son, has to give form, although it is possible to cite a number of ways of attributing initiatives to the Spirit without reference or at least with insufficient references to the Word. This is what Luther encountered in those whom he called 'fanatical enthusiasts' or *Schwärmer*.[5]

One of the most striking aspects of the contemporary scene has been a rediscovery of the charisms in our theology *de Ecclesia*. They reappeared officially for the first time in Pius XII's encyclical *Mystici Corporis* of 29 June

1943, in which it was said that 'it should not in any way be thought that this well ordered or, as it is called, "organic" structure of the body of the Church is completed or circumscribed exclusively within the degrees of the hierarchy or, as an opposite opinion claims, that it is formed simply of "charismatics", those men who are gifted with marvellous gifts (*prodigialibus*) and whose presence will never be lacking from the Church'.[6]

In the above encyclical letter, the charisms were taken in the sense of their rather more extraordinary forms. Pius XII's text is echoed in a later document, the Dogmatic Constitution on the Church *Lumen Gentium* of Vatican II.[7] The Council, however, dealt in a wider and generally much better way with the charisms of the Spirit, seeing them as dynamic principles given to all believers for the building up of the Church and the carrying out of the Church's mission.[8] The Church was not simply founded in the beginning — God continues without ceasing to build it up, which is, of course, the basic idea contained in 1 Cor 12.

Taking Paul, who created the term, as his point of departure, a disciple of Hans Küng, Gotthold Hasenhüttl, suggested in 1970 that the charisms were the 'principle of order' (*Ordnungsprinzip*) in the Church.[9] By 'order' Hasenhüttl does not mean the external organization of the Church as defined in the juridical sense. It is rather the principle that makes the Church as organism (or, as Pius XII expressed it: *organicam, ut aiunt*). It is the free power of Christ who builds up the organism of the Church. That power is the Spirit with Jesus Christ as the criterion. In this building up of the organism, each member has a place of service according to the gift that he or she has received. This is what Hasenhüttl calls the 'order of the community' (*Gemeindeordnung*; p. 99). The charism is 'a specific vocation resulting from the event of salvation (embracing time and eternity), which is carried out in the community which constitutes it and constantly builds it up and which serves our fellow-men in love' (p. 238). Elsewhere, the author calls the charisms 'the structure of the Church' and the community 'the place of the charisms' (p. 128).

Hasenhüttl does not, however, overlook the existence of instituted ministers. He points to the presence, at the time of St Paul, of a presbyteral organization of the Jerusalem type, that of the so-called elders. The pastoral epistles describe how the second generation of these elders developed. The so-called apostolic Fathers, Clement and Ignatius of Antioch, would seem to have no longer regarded the charisms as forming the community and to have considered those who had received such charisms as 'pneumatics' living from the Spirit, but only for themselves (p. 306). The Second Vatican Council rediscovered the charisms, but did not believe that they alone formed the structure of the Church. The Church had a double structure according to Vatican II — both hierarchical and charismatic — here Hasenhüttl cites the

Dogmatic Constitution *Lumen Gentium* 4 and 8 (p. 334). He seems to place the power of pastors above that of the charisms (and not only of the extraordinary charisms) for the purpose of judging them (p. 347). There is, in Hasenhüttl's opinion, a need for juridical structures in the Church, but rather at the level of auxiliary structures in those cases in which the one who has the function lacks the corresponding charism. This auxiliary structure should not, however, become fundamental and unique (p. 355). For Hasenhüttl, then, the ideal situation is that of a Church as a community made by charisms as services and not primarily of a Church as an organization and a hierarchy.

It is quite true that two principles were retained by Vatican II, which saw the Church as a society and as a communion.[10] I would also add that, according to the Council, the social structure of the Church is not primarily juridical, but sacramental. This is, in my opinion, essential. I would connect this with the relative duality on the one hand of the institution of the Church by the incarnate Word during his presence in the flesh and, on the other, of the permanent activity here and now of the glorified Lord, who is Spirit. I would not venture to draw attention now to the distinction which I have made in the past between structure and life, because it has been criticized for being inadequate.

Here I would suggest two ways in which this dual pattern of the two aspects of the life of the Church can perhaps be applied. In the case of the second way, which I shall consider below, there is, I think, more than mere analogy or similarity.

The first example is concerned with the relationship between the body of believers and that of the Church's pastors in the expression and preservation of revealed truth. Decisions, *horoi* that are valuable in themselves, have resulted from the ecumenical councils of the Church.[11] but increasing recognition is given now to the 'reception' of those decisions by Christians. This is something that brings us closer to the Orthodox concept of *sobornost*.[12] It is in fact all believers, the whole People of God as the Body of Christ with the indwelling of the Holy Spirit, who preserve the Tradition of the apostolic faith, whereas it is the pastoral *magisterium* which interprets, teaches and authentically formulates that Tradition.

Vatican II said this and Umberto Betti has provided an excellent commentary on the conciliar text,[13] pointing out that the service provided by the hierarchy, which enjoys a *charisma veritatis certum*, is carried out only *in medio ecclesiae*, that is, within the communion of the Church community. There are therefore two realities and the Council says that both tend towards a unity of feeling: *fiat Antistitum et fidelium conspiratio*.[14] Each believer makes a contribution in his place and according to his gifts. Betti believes that the non-hierarchical charisms that are given to each believer for the common good do not form a constitutive difference within the Church, but intervene exclusively at the level of activity. There is 'structure' and there is 'life'. It would be an oversimplification to say just 'Word' and 'Breath', because both are present in each part. What we have here, nevertheless, is an instance of the dialectical tension between the forms imposed by the founder and their internalization in those who believe.

The second example is provided by the contemporary life of the Church in France. It has often been pointed out that all the country's institutions are in a state of crisis — the universities, the armed forces, the legal system and the Church. There is an ever-decreasing number of priests and the age of those who are left is increasing alarmingly. The structural framework of dioceses, parishes, movements and associations has survived, but it no longer provides the setting for the whole vitality of the Church as it did in the past. Fewer and fewer people practise their faith[15] or even raise questions about God. France is slipping gently into calm indifference!

Yet, although we are living in what might be described as a comfortable desert, a Church is being constantly refashioned as the Gospel makes fresh springs rise again in the lives of men and women. Writing about the French Resistance, Louis Aragon said: 'Where I fall, the Fatherland is reborn' and the same could be said of the situation in France today. The Gospel and the Spirit are constantly rising again in hundreds, even thousands of springs from an underground source of water below the contemporary desert of France. These springs are giving new life, stimulating fresh initiatives and reshaping the attitudes of many members of the People of God and the Church.[16] They are an expression of the charisms or the talents which the Spirit is giving to so many people for the building up of the Body of Christ and which can be seen as the 'principle of order' of a Church that is being reborn from its foundations.

Many priests find this phenomenon disconcerting. What function will they have if such aspects of the Church are reborn or exist as the result of the activity of lay believers? In the past, they were accustomed to doing everything for the lay members of the Church, who were above all the objects of their ministry. Now, however, the members of communities of believers are the subjects of their own lives and of their existence as Church[17] — above all on the basis of the charisms and a new way of implementing the programme outlined in 1 Cor 12:4-30.

What place then, should ordained priests have now in this building up of a Church now taking place from its foundations and through the free movement of grace? Their task is, I think, to provide a link with the apostolic institution that comes from Christ, the founder of the new People of God. The ordination that he has received from his bishop in the communion of the *ecclesia* makes the priest a member of that chain of mission and ministry in which the Twelve were the first links. He is the presence in a certain sense of the bishop, who is himself the presence of the apostolic Body.[18] He is therefore qualified to link the community, which is living from its foundation, to the institution in its apostolicity and its Catholicity. The ordained minister therefore possesses in his own right the sacramental actions — the forgiveness of sins and the Eucharist — that were handed over to the Apostles. Every Christian can, however, admit another into the Church by baptism. The Church appears therefore to come both from the Word in his incarnation and from the Spirit — or the glorified Lord — who is unceasingly active both in men and women and in sacramental or juridical structures. Truly, God works with his two hands conjointly.

Notes

1   I would mention here L. Sartori, 'The Structure of Juridical and Charismatic Power in the Christian Community', *Concilium* 109 (November 1977), 56-66; J. Liebart, 'Communion spirituelle et institution dans l'Eglise avant le IVe siècle. Un sondage', *ACan* XXV (1981), 149-168; F. Hahn, 'Charisma und Amt. Die Diskussion über das kirchliche Amt im Lichte der neutestamentlichen Charismenlehre', *ZThK* 76 (1979), 419-449, written from the Protestant perspective.

2   Contributions were made, for example, by K. L. Schmidt, O. Linton, A. Fridrichsen and M. Goguel. See also F. M. Braun, *Aspects nouveaux du problème de l'Eglise* (Fribourg and Lyons, 1942), pp. 43ff., which can be supplemented by the German version *Neues Licht auf die Kirche* (Einsiedeln, 1946), pp. 70ff.

3   A.-L. Descamps, 'L'origine de l'institution ecclésiale selon le Nouveau Testament', *L'Eglise: institution et foi* (*Publications des Facultés universitaires Saint Louis* 14; Brussels, 1979), pp. 91-138; E. Lohfink, *Wie hat Jesus Gemeinde gewollt? Zur gesellschaftlichen Dimension des christlichen Glaubens* (Freiburg, 1982).

4   L. Boff, *Eglise en genèse. Les communautés de base réinventent l'Eglise* (Paris, 1978), pp. 79-80 and 84 [Eng. trans.: *Ecclesiogenesis* (Maryknoll, 1986)].

5   See *I Believe in the Holy Spirit* I (London and New York, 1983), pp. 138-139.

6   *AAS* 35 (1943), 200.

7   *Ecclesiam ... diversis donis hierarchicis et charismaticis (Spiritus Sanctus) instruit ac dirigit*, 'The Holy Spirit furnishes and directs the Church with various gifts, both hierarchical and charismatic': *Lumen Gentium* 4. See also the Decree on the Church's Missionary Activity *Ad Gentes Divinitus* 4, where this text is quoted.

8   See *Lumen Gentium* 12, 2; *Ad Gentes Divinitus* 23, 1 and 28, 1; Decree on the Apostolate of the Laity *Apostolicam Actuositatem* 3, 4. There have been numerous studies.

9   G. Hasenhüttl, *Charisma — Ordnungsprinzip der Kirche* (*Oekumenische Forschungen*, ed. H. Küng and J. Ratzinger, 5; Freiburg, 1970). A similar position can be found in Karl Barth.

10   See A. Acerbi, *Due ecclesiologie, ecclesiologia giuridica ed ecclesiologia di communione nella 'Lumen gentium'* (Bologna, 1975).

11   See D.-B. Dupuy, 'Le magistère de l'Eglise, service de la Parole', *L'infaillibilité de l'Eglise* (Chèvetogne, 1963), pp. 53-67.

12   See my study 'La "réception" comme réalité ecclésiologique', *RSPhTh* 56 (1972), 369-403.

13   U. Betti, 'Le magistère de l'Eglise au service de la Parole de Dieu: à propos du n° 10 de la Constitution dogmatique "Dei verbum" ', *Au service de la Parole de Dieu. Mélanges Mgr Charue* (Gembloux, 1969), pp. 245-261. *Charisma veritatis certum* is used in *Dei Verbum* 8, 2 in the sense of a charism of function, but there is no reference to Irenaeus, since the sense in which he uses it is disputed.

14   It is tempting to recall in this context the *sumpnoia* of which Basil speaks: *Ep.* 164, 1 (*PG* 32, 636).

15   The chaplain at one of France's great airports has told me that only seventy of the 15,000 people employed there regularly practise their faith. The national average is not the same, but the problem is still very great!

16   I would mention, for example, only the 150,000 voluntary catechists in France, the countless people involved in helping the poor, ex-prisoners, drug addicts, women in distress; the cases of lay people taking responsibility for parishes without priests and for chaplaincies; those who are trying to lead new evangelical ways of life. For the latter, see, for instance, 'Vie religieuse: nouveaux départs?', bulletin no. 92 of *Pro Mundi Vita* (Brussels, 1st term, 1983).

17   For a theology of members of churches as subjects, see Hervé Legrand, 'Le développement d'Eglises-sujets, une requête de Vatican II', G. Alberigo (ed.), *Les Eglises après Vatican II. Dynamisme et prospective* (*ThH* 61; Paris, 1981), pp. 149-184.

18   See the Decree on the Ministry and Life of Priests *Presbyterorum Ordinis* 2, 2-4; 5, 1; 6; 7. See also the Dogmatic Constitution *Lumen Gentium* 28.

6

The place of the Holy Spirit in Christology

I was trained in the Christology of Thomas Aquinas, which I loved.[1] I would summarize it as a theology of essential grace and the foundation of the doctrine of the Mystical Body. I still particularly love questions 7 and 8 of Part IIIa of the *Summa Theologiae*, but I have a better understanding now than I did then of the unsatisfactory nature of *ST* IIIa, qq. 1-60, which I have just reread, and the extent to which it has, despite its undeniable greatness, been susperseded. Thomas did more than simply define the ontological status of Christ. He was conscious of Christ's finality as the redeemer and the mediator of salvation *propter nos et propter nostram salutem*, for us and for our salvation. Thomas included within his theology a detailed and very careful examination of the various aspects, actions and events in the history of Christ from the Annunciation to the sitting at the right hand of the Father in judgement, studying these by combining the methods of symbolic understanding with those of Aristotelian philosophy.

Nowadays, we try to read Scripture in a more purely biblical and historical way. Thomas, however, like so many of the Fathers of the Church, saw Christ as having, from the moment of his conception, the fullness of grace, the use of his free will, infused knowledge, a vision of God and the glory, not of his body, but of his soul.[2] It is true that Thomas situates the Holy Spirit in the life of Christ, as I shall show below, but did he fully recognize the part that he played in Jesus' conception? That part was simply to form Christ's body in Mary's womb. But the idea of the hypostatic union with the Word was so exclusive that the *virtus Altissimi*, 'power of the Most High', of Lk 1:35 is taken to be Christ himself.[3]

Thomas' theology of created grace prevented him from developing a more complete understanding of the role of the Holy Spirit. He knew and in fact said that Christ was in his humanity full of the Holy Spirit,[4] and he also believed that Christ had those gifts which made him supremely sensitive to the movements of the Spirit.[5] He knew, moreover, that created grace

presupposes at its source the uncreated grace that the Holy Spirit in fact is.[6]
As we have already seen, Thomas believed that the Holy Spirit was, in the
Mystical Body, as it were the heart, the principle of life, from which the head
received its vitality, while controlling all the members. If there is a
communication of the fullness of grace from Christ to those members, that is,
to ourselves, it is only in a specific sense and not in an identical and numerical
sense that the grace is the same.[7] On the other hand, the first and uncreated
principle of that grace is *idem numero*, identically the same, in Christ and in
ourselves.[8]

Thomas, then, worked with the idea of created grace, which was a term
recently coined (1245). He began by postulating the grace of the union, which
is the hypostatic union itself, but only expresses the human and divine
ontology of Christ. Created grace was required if Christ was to be active in a
holy manner according to his humanity. That created grace was also a
necessary consequence for the grace of the union and, as we have already seen,
it was needed from the moment of Christ's conception.[9] The Holy Spirit was
presupposed, but Thomas spoke explicitly above all of created sanctifying
grace and the other charisms with which Christ functioned in a holy manner.
These were, according to Thomas, gifts that had come to him in their
fullness, at the moment of his conception, in such a way that they did not
increase (q. 7, a. 12).

I find Thomas' theology of Christ unsatisfactory now for two reasons. It is
true that he regarded both the Christology of the ontology of the incarnate
Word and soteriology as a single theme to be discussed within the framework
of the same treatise and that he also included a study of the aspects and actions
in the life of Christ within that framework. In that study, however, he gave
more attention to the aspect of descent, that is, the incarnation of the Word,
than to the aspect of reascent, in which the action of the Holy Spirit is
involved.[10]

Everything that had to be said about the first question was said at the
Council of Chalcedon, and this continued to dominate theology. But, as Fr
Smulders has pointed out, this meant that there was a danger of losing sight of
the messianic and saving work of God throughout the stages of the history of
salvation. It was the crisis of Monothelitism and its solution at the Lateran
Council of 649 and the Third Council of Constantinople in 680-681 which
drew attention to the fact that Christ had been called in the truth of his human
nature to fulfil himself and his mission as Messiah and Saviour through
conscious and free activity in which the movement of the Spirit was present.[11]

Thomas reflected about these aspects in the history of Christ, but not in a
completely historical way. Everything was established at the time of the
incarnation (the Annunciation) and what happened after then was a
manifestation for others. The position adopted by the early Fathers is

undoubtedly very similar.[12] What is absent from this presentation is, it seems to me, a full recognition of the historical character of the economy of salvation. This was accomplished, in my view, in a series of events which were situated in time and which provided something new once they had occurred. There were *kairoi*, certain established 'times' that were suitable for this kind of event to take place (see, for example, Mk 1:15; Gal 4:4; Eph 1:10). Jesus himself frequently spoke of his 'hour', saying that it had or had not yet come.[13] I believe that the historical stages marked by the events that I shall review briefly below were authentic qualitative moments in which God's communication of himself in Jesus Christ and in a very real sense also to Jesus Christ was accomplished. There were successive comings of the Holy Spirit over Jesus in his quality as 'Christ the Saviour'. This is, in my view, implied by the New Testament texts that I consider below.

The first two chapters of Luke's Gospel mention the Spirit and his interventions many times. As soon as the Christological aspect of the divine economy begins, the Spirit is at work. The first decisive event of that economy after the virginal conception is John's baptism of Jesus. This, in Mark's Gospel, is the beginning of the Good News — the Gospel. In the three synoptic gospels, a voice from heaven declares that Jesus is God's beloved Son, the one whom he has chosen. These words recall those of Ps 2:7, which in turn go back to the idea of royal messianism and are reminiscent of Nathan's prophecy to David (2 Sam 7:14) and the beginning of the song of the Servant, which continues with the words: 'I have put my Spirit on him' (Is 42:1).[14]

The Spirit also descends on Jesus in the form of a dove. This is a Trinitarian manifestation, an investiture and a consecration. Light is thrown on the meaning of this event in Peter's discourse in the house of Cornelius in Acts: 'The word which was proclaimed throughout all Judaea, beginning from Galilee after the baptism which John preached: how God anointed Jesus of Nazareth with the Holy Spirit and with power, how he went about doing good and healing all that were oppressed by the devil, for God was with him' (Acts 10:37-38).

This is the anointing which makes Jesus the 'Christ' or Messiah. The New Testament knows of no other anointing.[15] Many of the Fathers as well as the scholastics and Thomas Aquinas situated this anointing at Jesus' conception and attributed it to the Word,[16] calling it the hypostatic union. In their opinion, Jesus possessed everything from that moment onwards. They consequently regarded his baptism as no more than a manifestation pointing in addition to the truth of Christian baptism. The narrowness and rigidity of this view is avoided by Hilary of Poitiers, who does not, however, deny its dogmatic position, in his claim that Christ was already the Son of God, but was born at his baptism to a new quality as Son and that the truth of this claim is verified by the text of the second psalm.[17]

What we have, then, in the anointing of Jesus at the time of his baptism is a new act in which his divine sonship was made present — the act that made him and declared him to be 'Christ'. Before that event, it was not known that he had those gifts which he was able from then onwards to use.[18] He was able to express in an entirely new way, in the perspective of his mission, his consciousness, at the human level, of his quality as the Son of God and of his condition as the Servant.

Immediately after his baptism, Jesus was led by the Spirit into the desert, where he was tempted (Mt 4:1; Mk 1:12; Lk 4:1). That temptation, which is the first event following Jesus' messianic baptism, is also concerned with his consciousness of being the Son and the Servant. This is clear from the fact that the temptation in the desert is followed at once by Jesus' proclamation: 'The time (ho kairos) is fulfilled and the kingdom of God is at hand' (Mk 1:15). Jesus came, in other words, to proclaim and to inaugurate the kingdom of God. He healed those who were held in subjugation by the devil. His first act was one in which he confronted the counter-kingdom. This confrontation took place immediately following what had been made known to him at the time of his baptism, namely, his condition as the Son and the Servant. 'If you are the Son of God' is what the tempter, who knows only one temptation, to 'be like God' (see Gen 3:5), suggests to him. 'If you are the Son of God', the tempter urged him, work miracles! Make use of your power!

Jesus knew that he was the Servant and that he had come to do the Father's will (Heb 10:5-9). At the beginning of his ministry in Galilee, where he went 'in the power of the Spirit' (Lk 4:14), he went to Nazareth. In the synagogue there, he found the song of the Servant. This proclaimed and summarized the whole of his ministry: 'The Spirit of the Lord is upon me, because he has anointed me to preach good news to the poor. He has sent me to proclaim release to the captives and recovering of sight to the blind, to set at liberty those who are oppressed, to proclaim the acceptable year of the Lord' (Lk 4:18-19 = Is 61:1-2 and 58:6).

Jesus did not often speak about the Spirit. There are relatively few references to him in the first three gospels,[19] and many exegetes retain even fewer as a result of their investigations. However, the references to the Spirit are very characteristic. They show that Jesus was led by the Spirit in his struggle against the demon and empowered by the Spirit in his initiation of the kingdom of God. Jesus' reply to the 'Jews', who suspected him of driving out demons by Beelzebul, their leader, was: 'If it is by the Spirit of God that I cast out demons, then the kingdom of God has come upon you'.[20] Peter, moreover, spoke of healings; these were not only a very important aspect of Jesus' saving activity, but also a sign of the coming of the kingdom (see Lk 10:9-11). It was because the Spirit was acting in him that Jesus was able to manifest the sovereign mercy and loving kindness of God, which is his kingdom.

The Spirit also made him tremble with joy when he gave thanks to the Father for all that he had revealed in his loving kindness (Lk 10:21-22; cf. Mt 11:25-27). What an unobtrusive glimpse of the prayer of Jesus that nevertheless plays such an important part in the gospels and particularly that of Luke!

Is the Holy Spirit involved in Heb 9:14, which refers to 'the blood of Christ, who through the eternal spirit offered himself without blemish to God'?[21] Many authors think so and it is also cautiously suggested in the words *cooperante Spiritu Sancto* ('by the work of the Holy Spirit') contained in one of the communion prayers of the Roman liturgy. There is evidence of the existence of this prayer in the ninth century and it has been retained among other such prayers as one of the richest and most profound of its kind.

The fourth gospel, which, even more than the other gospels, was composed in the light of the Easter event, shows Christ not only as possessing the Spirit, but also as giving and, in the last discourses, as promising the Paraclete. Promising the gift of the Spirit is an aspect of Jesus' life in the flesh and also even that of John the Baptist, but effective communication of the Spirit is above all an activity of the glorified Lord. These two aspects are distinguished by Paul:

> the gospel concerning his Son, who was descended from David according to the flesh and designated Son of God in power according to the Spirit of holiness by his resurrection from the dead, Jesus Christ our Lord (Rom 1:3-4).[22]

Even in the flesh, then, as a descendant of David, Jesus was already the Son of God. God told him at his baptism: 'You are my Son'. He was, however, that Son in weakness, that is, in the state of kenosis referred to in the hymn found in Phil 2:6ff. He was condemned and died in ignominy, but, by raising him from the dead, God proclaimed that he who had been condemned and abandoned on the cross was his Son even in his humanity. Through the single act of his resurrection and glorification, Jesus was established in a new state as the Son of God, that is, with power. It was by God (the Father) that Jesus was raised from the dead.[23] It was, however, according to the Holy Spirit that this took place, and even through (*dia*) the Spirit in the case of our own resurrection as the consequence of Christ's (see Rom 8:11).

In 1 Pet 3:18 and 1 Tim 3:16, which reproduces an early Christian hymn, the two aspects distinguished by Paul are divided between the flesh and the Spirit: 'being put to death in the flesh but made alive in the Spirit'. On the other hand, 'the Spirit and power (are) indissolubly related'.[24] Our body of flesh is asthenic, whereas our resurrection body — our 'spiritual body' — is full of power. The glorified Christ — the eschatological Adam — did not

simply become a spiritual body. He became a 'life-giving spirit' (1 Cor
15:42-45). Having given his body of flesh as a sacrifice, Jesus received a
spiritualized and glorified body, which was a source of life. Having descended
to the lowest, he (re-)ascended to the highest level.

This great theology is expressed in Acts in the addresses given by Peter on
the day of Pentecost and by Paul at Antioch in Pisidia:

> Peter: This Jesus God raised up, and of that we are all witnesses. Being
> therefore exalted at the right hand of God, and having received from the
> Father the promise of the Holy Spirit, he has poured out this which you
> see and hear. For David did not ascend into the heavens, but he himself
> says, 'The Lord said to my Lord, Sit at my right hand, till I make thy
> enemies a stool for thy feet' (Ps 110:1) (Acts 2:32-35).

> Paul: And we bring you the good news that what God promised to the
> fathers, this he has fulfilled to us their children by raising Jesus, as also it is
> written in the second psalm, 'Thou art my Son, today I have begotten thee'
> (Ps 2:7) (Acts 13:32-33).

The following text from the Epistle to the Hebrews (1:5-6) should also be
added to these two testimonies:

> For to what angel did God ever say, 'Thou art my Son, today I have
> begotten thee' (Ps 2:7)? Or again, 'I will be to him a father and he shall be
> to me a son' (2 Sam 7:14)? And again, when he brings the first-born into
> the world, he says, 'Let all God's angels worship him' (Dt 32:43, Greek
> text).

The words 'when he brings the first-born into the world' might well lead us
to think that the author is referring to the incarnation of Christ.[25] The
context, however, is concerned with Christ's glorification and especially the
verses immediately preceding the text cited above (1:3b-4) have that in mind:
'When he had made purification for sins, he sat down at the right hand of the
Majesty on high, having become as much superior to angels as the name he
has obtained is more excellent than theirs'. Several of the verses that follow
also deal with Christ in glory (1:13; 2:9-10).

The parallelism between these ideas and their continuation on the one hand
and Rom 1:3-4 on the other has been emphasized by J. Dupont, who points
out that

> the title of Son is given in the Epistle to the Hebrews and in that to the
> Romans to Christ within the context of statements about the period

preceding his glorification — God 'has spoken to us by a Son' (Heb 1:2). This title is, however, not fully applied to Christ until after he has entered into glory. It is only then that he becomes 'superior to angels' and that this superiority is fully transferred to the name that is given to him... The name of Son, which shows that Christ is more excellent than the angels, is not said by the author of Hebrews to be his because of his origin. It was given to him, according to that author, at the moment of his exaltation.[26]

The Epistle to the Hebrews is concerned throughout with Christ's priesthood. This means that he was also a priest in his weakness (see 4:15; 9:14). That priesthood was, however, brought to its fulfilment (5:9; 7:28) when he was enthroned in heaven. 'Christ did not exalt himself to be made a high priest, but was appointed by him who said to him, "Thou art my Son, today I have begotten thee" (Ps 2:7): as he says also in another place, "Thou art a priest for ever, after the order of Melchizedek" (Ps 110:4)' (5:5-6). The author explains this assimilation to Melchizedek by pointing out that the latter appears 'without father or mother or genealogy' (7:3).

A. Vanhoye has provided the following commentary on this passage:

> It is possible to say of the risen Christ that he was a man 'without father or mother or genealogy' because his resurrection was a new begetting of his human nature, in which neither a human father nor a human mother intervened, with the result that he was a 'first-born' (Heb 1:6) without an act of begetting. If Peter was able to say that Christians were 'born anew through the resurrection of Jesus Christ from the dead' (1 Pet 1:3), surely the same could also be said all the more of the risen Christ himself.[27]

It is not possible to give the texts that we have been studying here their full value simply by considering the purely ontological structure of the incarnate Word. Two aspects and similarly two conditions in Christ's quality of Son of God can be distinguished in a *historical* Christology. He was the Son of God *in forma servi*, that is, in the flesh. As such he received the Spirit, was made holy by him and acted through him, especially in his struggle against the demon. Following his resurrection, he was constituted according to the Holy Spirit as the Son of God with power. He was 'seated at the right hand of God' and was assimilated to him even in his humanity. From that moment onwards, then, and from heaven, he gives the Spirit. Acts 2:33 should be reread in this context.[28] Jesus' humanity, united from the very beginning to the person of the Word, has been brought to the condition of a Son of God humanity. Having received that condition of glory (Jn 17:5), Jesus sends the Paraclete 'from the Father' (15:26).[29]

Jesus is Son in several ways. He is Son by an eternal begetting — he is 'begotten, not made' — and therefore he is the *Monogenitus* or *Monogenēs*. In a theology that is concerned with the economy of salvation, however, we have to take seriously the texts in which the quotation from Ps 2:7 — 'Thou art my Son, today I have begotten thee' — is applied in history. The first case of this is, as we have seen, the annunciation of the angel to Mary: 'He will be called ... the Son of God' (Lk 1:35). The second is at the theophany when Jesus was baptized in the Jordan (Mt 3:17; Mk 1:11; Lk 3:22). The third reference is connected with the resurrection and exaltation (Acts 13:33; Heb 1:5; 5:5).

These are all moments when Jesus was not simply proclaimed the 'Son of God', but when he in fact became that Son in a new way. He became the Son of God not from the point of view of his hypostatic quality or from that of his ontology as the incarnate Word, but from that of God's offer of grace and the successive moments in the history of salvation. That is the point of view according to which Jesus was destined to be — and, what is more, to be *for us* — the Messiah and Saviour in the form of a Servant and then Lord, taken up to the right hand of God. As Peter said on the day of Pentecost: 'God has made (*epoiēsen*) him both Lord and Christ, this Jesus whom you crucified' (Acts 2:36).

Jesus is then regarded no longer as the *Monogenēs*, but as the *Prōtotokos*, that is, the first-born to divine and glorious life with regard to that multitude of brethren who are called and predestined to be conformed to his model. There is one begetting (and even two) of Jesus as the first-born Son, that is, as having us in mind and including us in the divine sonship. Like him in his humanity, we shall not be fully sons until the glorious transfiguration of the resurrection, but, like him too, we are also already sons according to the first-fruits of this life and groaning inwardly.

For us as for Jesus, that quality of Son was, in both its stages, the work of the Spirit who, as the Third in the intra-divine life (in the equality of consubstantiality), is the agent of sonship as the effect of grace and the reality of holy life in the divine economy. The whole of our filial life is inspired by the Spirit (Rom 8:14-17; Gal 4:6).

In dealing with Jesus, it is important to avoid Adoptionism. I am of the opinion that he was ontologically the Son of God by a hypostatic union from the moment of his conception and that he was also from that moment onwards the Temple of the Holy Spirit and made holy in his humanity by that Spirit. I am, however, anxious to do justice to the successive moments or stages in the history of our salvation and to bring out the realism of all the relevant New Testament texts. For these reasons, then, I would suggest that there were two 'actuating' moments[30] in the *virtus* or effectiveness of the Spirit in Jesus insofar as he was constituted — and not simply proclaimed — by God as the Messiah and Saviour and then as Lord.

I would like to say something here about the relationship between these 'economic' aspects of sonship and the eternal Sonship of Christ. It is possible to formulate the question as follows: We know that Jesus Christ is God. But how is God Jesus Christ? Making an initial approach to this question in the confidence that there will be general agreement, I would say that the Word was conceived *incarnandum* and even *crucifigendum, glorificandum, caput multorum Dei filiorum* — that, at his conception, he had to be made flesh, crucified and glorified as the head of many sons of God. But what I have said above leads me to add that, in this respect, the Word proceeds *a Patre Spirituque*, from the Father and the Spirit, since the latter intervenes in all the acts or moments in the history of the Word *incarnate*. If all the *acta et passa* of the divine economy are traced back to the eternal begetting of the Word, then the Spirit has to be situated at that point.

Karl Barth pointed out that to adhere, without making any subtle distinctions, to the principle according to which the economic Trinity is the same as the immanent Trinity and *vice versa* would be to contradict the *Filioque*. He rejected that conclusion, basing his argument on the fact that the actions of the Spirit in the life of Christ did not constitute the latter's existence, whereas, in the case of the Trinitarian processions, it was a case of making him exist. I have also pointed out elsewhere that this *'vice versa'* has to be treated with some reserve if we are to do justice to the transcendence of the intra-Trinitarian mystery.[31]

Because of the way in which both Paul and John speak about Jesus Christ as (already) existing in God independently of his coming in the flesh at a certain moment in history, I am obliged to ask my question in a more radical form. First of all, I shall briefly review the most important testimonies.

Some texts can be interpreted as referring to a simple predestination: 1 Tim 3:16 — 'He was manifested in the flesh' — and 1 Pet 1:18-20 — 'You were ransomed . . . with the precious blood of Christ, like that of a lamb without blemish or spot. He was (pre-)destined before the foundation of the world, but was made manifest at the end of the times for your sake'. Rev 13:8 is also frequently cited, although the *Traduction oecuménique* [like RSV, JB and NJB] connects the words 'the foundation of the world' not with the sacrifice of the lamb, but with the writing of the names of believers in the book of life.

However, there are many affirmations of pre-existence. The earliest text is Phil 2:5ff.: 'Christ Jesus, who, though he was in the form of God . . . '. Other texts are those attributed to Jesus himself in the fourth gospel, especially: 'I speak of what I have seen with my Father' (Jn 8:38), ' . . . in thy love for me before the foundation of the world' (17:24) and 'Before Abraham was, I am' (8:58). Particular attention is given to Johannine statements made in terms of the 'Son of man': he has descended from heaven and will reascend into heaven

(3:13; 6:62). There is also Jesus' reply to the high priest in the synoptic gospels (see Mt 26:64; Mk 14:62; Lk 22:69).

The theme of Christ as the 'image of God' is present but not prominent in 2 Cor 4:4, but it occurs with splendour and solemnity in Col 1:15-20, which may be a very early Christian hymn,[32] and in Heb 1:2-3. Christ, who obtained deliverance and forgiveness of sins for us and through whom God has spoken, is the 'image of the invisible God' and the first-born of every creature. Everything is created through him and for him (see 1 Cor 8:6). Everything has firmness in him. He was appointed to inherit everything. As André Feuillet has pointed out, these texts apply to Christ the privileges of eternal and creative wisdom (see Prov 8:22ff.; Sir 24:5-6). It is Jesus Christ who is said in these texts to have existed in God before manifesting himself in our history.

It is not enough simply to make a distinction between the eternal Word and the man–God of the incarnation. Scripture speaks of the pre-existence of the latter. Several theologians have given serious consideration to this question; I will cite only three.

The chapter in his *Church Dogmatics* on God's gratuitous election is certainly one of the most original that Karl Barth ever wrote and possibly one that was closest to his own heart.[33] I hope that the following summary of the sequence of the ideas contained in that chapter is a faithful reproduction of his thought.

God is real and actual. He is not a God constructed by metaphysical reasoning. He should only be understood in the sense in which he has revealed himself (p. 195). He is essentially 'the Father of our Lord Jesus Christ' (p. 4). His work of creation and both his choice of a being different from himself as the object of his love and his drawing him and taking him to himself so that he is no longer God without him are acts of love and gratuitous generosity (p. 9).

Free and gratuitous choice or election, then, comes first and has to be considered first — even before creation, for which it is the reason, and before sin. This election is, moreover, an election of Jesus Christ, who is true God and true man. In him, it is also an election of Israel and the Church. Freely and through grace, 'God wanted to be Jesus Christ' (p. 104).

But Jesus Christ is not simply the object of this election.[34] He is the subject of it. He is also not simply the 'chosen' one. He is the 'one who chooses'. Barth says: 'Jesus Christ is the God who chooses. Jesus Christ is the man chosen' (p. 106). He is, moreover, that subject in unity with the Father and the Spirit (p. 108).

This free choice has two consequences — for man it means life, but for God, in Jesus Christ, it means the condemnation and death which man deserved and which God has taken on himself in man's place.[35] God's faithfulness to his love, however, obtained life and glory for Jesus.

At the heart of this theology is an absolute affirmation that has always struck me very forcibly in Luther, namely that Jesus Christ is God and that the Son of God is Jesus Christ. Barth refuses to recognize any other meaning in the two verses of the Gospel of John than Jesus Christ. I have myself witnessed the vigour with which Barth rejected any consideration of the Word other than Jesus Christ.

A Thomist is, however, bound to object to this. Thomas Aquinas in fact asks whether the statement: 'A man is God' is true. His reply is: 'Yes', because of the hypostatic union, since the hypostasis is that of the Word of God. But he adds that this is not exact *reduplicative*, if 'man' is taken as such.[36] Thomas always speaks *formaliter*. The claim to attribute hypostasis to the Word is one thing and that of nature is another. Nature was only assumed and united in time. Is it therefore possible to speak, in the case of the Word, of an existence *before* human nature was assumed? Thomas' answer is 'no', because 'before' is not meaningful in the context of the present and eternity of God. The eternal begetting of the Word, the Son, has, as its end, the Word, the Son, assuming the humanity of Jesus, which, in our own time or history, was brought about in the Annunciation. Mary, to whom that Annunciation was made, is therefore also eternally chosen and destined together with the Word. That is why, in the celebration of the mysteries of salvation in both the Eastern and the Western liturgies, those texts which refer to divine Wisdom are applied to her.[37] This, however, is something to which Barth devotes no attention at all, although it is a very profound aspect of this question.

We may therefore conclude that it is possible to speak of the Word *without* Jesus' assumption of humanity, although it is not possible to speak of the existence of that Word *before* the incarnation. This is the condition by which justice is done to the difference between the necessary mystery of the Tri-unity of God and the free mystery of his election of grace. Barth was aware of that difference and affirmed it.

It is true that the mystery of the Trinity can only be known through the economy. Are we therefore bound to conclude that we do not have to look for an eternal Son as distinct from Jesus of Nazareth? The formula is ambiguous. History has shown and Barth has admitted that the true and full meaning of the economy can only be preserved if we also include the theology, and the true and full meaning of Jesus Christ only if the eternal Word, the Son, is affirmed. Contemporary exegetes, however, can hardly be expected to follow the same approach that was followed by Christian thinkers from the second to the fifth century. They prefer to confine themselves to what Scripture in fact says. Oscar Cullmann and Pierre Benoît have done this.

Cullmann has studied the extra-biblical origins and uses of the title 'Son of man' and the way in which it is used in the New Testament and, taking this as his point of departure, has accepted the 'pre-existence' of Jesus as heavenly man, that is as man–God, in the sense that he achieved a perfect likeness with God.[38] According to Cullmann, Jesus came in the flesh (Jn 1:14),[39] that is to say, in our sinful humanity, which had lost that likeness, in order to give that likeness back to man. He was therefore the second Adam, the perfect human image of God and the head of a new humanity. In Jesus, heavenly man, who is the divine prototype of humanity, became incorporated into sinful humanity so that he might, through his obedience and his suffering, deliver humanity from its sins. When he had fulfilled the mission entrusted to man to be the image of God, he reascended in glory into heaven. Cullmann concludes his study with these words, which do not seem to have convinced his fellow-theologians:

> It would be still more important if a modern theologian would undertake to build a Christology entirely on the New Testament idea of the Son of Man. Not only would such a Christology be entirely oriented toward the New Testament and go back to Jesus' self-designation; it would also have the advantage of putting the logically insoluable problem of the two natures of Christ on a level where the solution becomes visible; the pre-existent Son of Man, who is with God already at the very beginning and exists with him as his image, is *by his very nature* divine man. From this point of view the whole toilsome discussion which dominated the earlier Christological controversies actually becomes superfluous.[40]

Pierre Benoît[41] begins by reviewing the texts, some of which I have considered in this chapter. He then goes on to say:

> This New Testament way of thinking and speaking confronts us with a problem and obliges us to re-examine our own. We should be very careful here. Our task is not to call the divine and the human natures of Jesus Christ into question or to throw doubt on their union in the one person who is the Word. Even if it is not expressed in that way in the New Testament, that dogmatic formula is perfectly valid and its philosophical concepts express a certain datum of Revelation. It is therefore of faith.
>
> The real question is this: Was the union of the divine and the human that took place at the moment of the Annunciation an absolute beginning, before which the Word subsisted alone within the Trinity? Or was it not preceded by a mysterious but real situation in which the future Man–God was already pre-existing, albeit in a different mode of existence from our own? If that was the case, how are we to think of that superior mode of existence that is neither a mode of pure divine and transcendent Being, nor that of the man Jesus after his birth on earth?

In his attempt to answer this question, Benoît does not follow the idea of 'heavenly man', but rather looks among Jewish and biblical ideas for an affirmation of an original type of existence that will enable him to attribute to Christ a created pre-existence other than that of the person of the eternal Son. He finds, for example, the idea of the spiritual but quite real presence of the rock, which, according to St Paul (1 Cor 10:4), accompanied the Israelites during the exodus. This existence is comparable to what the Jews had attributed to the Torah since the dawn of time; or the existence of the Son of man in the book of Daniel; or the existence of the creative and guiding Wisdom of God.

These are all spiritual realities that were already really existing with God before being manifested among men. They go back to a lasting framework of duration that transcends our earthly time. Benoît therefore concludes that 'before immersing himself in our human time, Jesus was already in existence as a whole Being, both man and God, in a time which is supremely real, but is distinct from our own, although it is not for that reason the pure eternity of God'. The sacramental reality also goes back, in Benoît's opinion, to the same kind of lasting duration and includes the historical event in the past — the Passion of Christ — present grace and the promised eschatological fulfilment in the future.

Most theologians have a different interpretation of sacramental time from Benoît's and very few would follow him in his hypothesis about pre-existence. I will personally do no more than simply echo the words of Louis Bouyer: 'It is in time that God makes Himself man, i.e. it is in a definite moment of time that our humanity is assumed. But as far as He is concerned, He assumes it eternally. Then the Father eternally generates His Son, not only as before His incarnation but also as the Word made flesh'.[42]

Eternity, then, is the here and now. I will end with these words of Karl Barth: 'From the very beginning, it was God's will to give himself in favour of man, in the concrete aspect of unity in his own Son or of his Word with the man Jesus of Nazareth' (p. 185).

Notes

1   I was taught by C.-V. Héris, the essential elements of whose work will be found in his book *Le mystère du Christ* (1928). In addition to this, I frequently examined Thomas' commentaries on Paul and John. M.-J. Guillou has made an excellent use of these commentaries in *Le Christ et l'Eglise. Théologie du mystère* (Paris, 1963).

2   From the moment of his conception, the fullness of grace (*ST* IIIa, q. 34, a. 1; this cannot increase: q. 7, a. 12), the use of his free will (q. 34, a. 2), merit (a. 3), a vision of God (a. 4) and the glory of his soul (q. 45, a. 1; q. 54, a. 3).

3 *ST* IIIa, q. 32, a. 1, ad 1 and 2; a. 2.

4 See *ST* IIa IIae, q. 14, a. 1: *Christus operabatur quaedam humanitus... et quaedam divinitus, scilicet daemones ejiciendo, mortuos suscitando et alia hujusmodi, quae quidem agebat et per virtutem propriae divinitatis et per operationem Spiritus Sancti quo secundum humanitatem erat repletus,* 'Christ performed certain actions in a human manner... and certain things in a divine manner, that is to say, driving out demons, restoring the dead to life and other similar things which he carried out in this way both by the power of his own divinity and by the working of the Holy Spirit, with whom he was filled according to his humanity'. See also *Comm. in 1 Cor.* c. 15, lect. 7: *Sicut Adam consecutus est perfectionem sui esse per animam, ita et Christus perfectionem sui esse, in quantum homo, per Spiritum Sanctum,* 'Just as Adam attained perfection of his being through his soul, so too did Christ achieve perfection of his being, as a man, through the Holy Spirit'.

5 See, for example, *ST* IIIa, q. 7, a. 5; q. 11, a. 1, ad 3.

6 *De Ver.* q. 24, a. 14; *ST* Ia IIae, q. 110, a. 1; IIIa, q. 2, a. 10; q. 7, a. 13.

7 Even grace *secundum essentiam*: *ST* IIIa, q. 8, a. 5.

8 *In III Sent.* d. 13, q. 2, a. 1, ad 2; *De Ver.* q. 29, a. 4; *Comm. in ev. Ioan.* c. 1, lect. 9 and 10; *ST* IIa IIae, q. 188, a. 3, ad 3.

9 *ST* IIIa, q. 6, a. 6; q. 7, a. 13; q. 34, a. 1.

10 *ST* IIIa, q. 34, a. 1, ad 1.

11 P. Smulders, 'Développement de la christologie dans le dogme et le Magistère', *Mysterium Salutis* 10 (Paris, 1974), pp. 235-350.

12 For the baptism of Jesus, see, for example, Justin Martyr, *Dial.* 88, 8 and 103, 6; Athanasius, *Contra Arian.* I, 47 and 48 (*PG* 26, 108C-109A and 112C-113A).

13 See Jn 2:4; 7:30; 8:20; 12:23; 13:1; 17:1.

14 J. Dupont, 'Filius meus es tu. L'interprétation du Ps II, 7 dans le Nouveau Testament', *RSR* 35 (1948), 522-543.

15 I. de la Potterie, 'L'onction du Christ', *NRT* 80 (1958), 225-252.

16 References will be found in my *I Believe in the Holy Spirit* I (London and New York, 1983), pp. 19-22. Thomas Aquinas also wrote: *Christus spirituali baptismate non indigebat, qui a principio suae conceptionis gratia Spiritu Sancti repletus fuit,* 'Christ, who was from the very beginning, when he was conceived, filled with the grace of the Holy Spirit, did not require spiritual baptism'; *ST* IIIa, q. 39, a. 2. See also a. 6, which deals with the symbolism of the dove.

17 Hilary of Poitiers, *Tract. in Ps. 2*, II, 29. Cited by J. Dupont, *op. cit.*, 526.

18 Hence the astonishment of Jesus' fellow-citizens (Lk 4:22; Mt 13:54-56; Mk 6:1ff.).

19 I lately studied J. D. G. Dunn, *Jesus and the Spirit. A Study of the Religious and Charismatic Experience of Jesus and the First Christians as Reflected in the New Testament* (Philadelphia, 1975), but I lent it, together with several other books, and it has not yet been returned. See also G. Beasley-Murray, 'Jesus and the Spirit', *Mélanges Bibliques en hommage au R. P. Béda Rigaux* (Gembloux, 1970), pp. 463-479, who points out that, although everyone believes that love is Jesus' central theme, he only mentions it explicitly twice in the synoptic gospels.

20 Mt 12:28. In the parallel text, Lk 11:20, the reading is: 'If it is by the finger of

God'. Which, then, is the earlier of the two texts? It is obvious that they are equivalents.

21 See *DThC* V, p. 222; H. Mühlen, *Mysterium Salutis* 13 (Paris, 1972), pp. 212ff.; A. Vanhoye, *De epistola ad Hebreos. Sectio Centralis (c. 8-9)* Rome, 1966), p. 158, and *Prêtres anciens, prêtres nouveaux selon le Nouveau Testament* (Paris, 1980), pp. 223 note 45, 256 note 47. C. Spicq, *Epître aux Hébreux* (1977), pp. 258-259, on the other hand, and most other exegetes think that all that is involved here is the aspect of eternity possessed by Christ in his being.

22 M. Hengel, *The Son of God* (London, 1976), pp. 59ff., thinks that this is a very early confession of faith, almost certainly Palestinian and prior to St Paul. Whereas Paul has *Kurios* 184 times, he only has *huios theou* fifteen times (p. 7).

23 See Rom 8:11; 1 Cor 6:14; 2 Cor 4:14; Eph 1:19-20; Acts 2:32; 5:30; 13:30, 33.

24 W. Grundmann, 'dunamai/dunamis', *TDNT* II, p. 301.

25 See W. Michaelis, 'prōtotokos', *TDNT* VI, p. 880.

26 J. Dupont, *op. cit.* (note 14), p. 537.

27 A. Vanhoye, *Prêtres anciens, op. cit.* (note 21), p. 178.

28 See the detailed analyses in M. Gourgues, *A la droite de Dieu. Résurrection de Jésus et actualisation du Ps 110,1 dans le Nouveau Testament* (*EtB*; Paris, 1978), especially pp. 163ff., 209ff.

29 In John's Gospel, the Spirit must be given when Jesus is glorified (Jn 7:39). Without looking for pointless subtle distinctions, I would say that it seems that this glorification should be seen as a process with its own duration and its own special moments. For John, it begins with the Passion. On the cross, Jesus 'gave up his breath (spirit)' (19:30) and on the day of his resurrection he gave his *pneuma* to the apostles (20:22). On the other hand, however, he told Mary Magdalene on the same day: 'I have not yet ascended to the Father' (20:17). Would he be not yet sitting at the right hand of the Father in that, though already risen from the dead, he was still appearing on earth? He had to send the Paraclete from the Father. F. Porsch's reply to this difficulty, *Pneuma und Wort. Ein exegetischer Beitrag zur Pneumatologie des Johannesevangeliums* (Frankfurt, 1974), pp. 275-276, is to say that Jesus gave the *pneuma* on the cross and on Easter evening, but not yet as the Paraclete whom he had promised in the farewell discourses. This was the beginning of the gift of what had been promised, as the cross and the resurrection are the beginning of Jesus' glorification.

30 L. F. Ladaria, 'Cristología del Logos y cristología del Espíritu', *Greg* 61 (1980), 353-360, approves of this term.

31 See my *I Believe in the Holy Spirit op. cit.* (note 16), III, pp. 11-18. I quote Karl Rahner, who follows Barth here, on p. 13.

32 André Feuillet has examined the hymn with the greatest precision in *Le Christ Sagesse de Dieu d'après le épîtres pauliniennes* (*EtB*; Paris, 1966), pp. 163-273.

33 I quote Karl Barth here from the (praiseworthy) Fr. trans.: *Dogmatique* II: *La doctrine de Dieu* II (Geneva, 1958), §§32 and 33, pp. 1-204 [Eng. trans.: *Church Dogmatics* II: 2 (Edinburgh, 1957), pp. 1-194]. Barth praises an article by Pierre Maury, 'Election et Foi', *FV* (April-May 1936).

34 A sharp criticism of Thomas Aquinas, who applies predestination only to the humanity of Christ. This is not wrong, but it is not enough.

35 'The obedience required of Jesus and to which he testifies is in fact nothing other than his eagerness to take on himself the rejection that others have to bear and to suffer what they have had to suffer themselves' (p. 127); 'The eternal will of God in choosing Jesus Christ is his will to sacrifice himself in favour of man, whom he has created' (p. 169); 'God wanted to be the loser so that man would be the winner' (p. 170).

36 Thomas Aquinas, *ST* IIIa q. 16, a. 2 and 11.

37 I feel quite at ease with the Orthodox Mariology of Alexis Kniazeff, 'Mariologie biblique et Liturgie byzantin', *Irén.* 28 (1955), 268-289, and published separately (Chèvetogne, 1955). See also L. Bouyer, *Le trône de la Sagesse. Essai sur la signification du culte marial* (Paris, 1957).

38 O. Cullmann, *The Christology of the New Testament* (London, 1959), chapter on 'Jesus the Son of Man', pp. 137-192.

39 Following J. Héring, Cullmann observes that John does not say that Jesus became 'man' — he was already man.

40 O. Cullmann, *op. cit.*, p. 192.

41 P. Benoît, 'Préexistence et Incarnation', *RB* 77 (1970), 5-29; repr. in *Exégèse et Théologie* IV (Paris, 1982), pp. 11-61.

42 L. Bouyer, *The Eternal Son. A Theology of the Word of God and Christology* (Huntington, Indiana, 1978), p. 401. It is surprising that Bouyer, who cites and discusses so many authors, should make no [detailed] reference to Barth. He shows himself, however, to be very close to the latter's point of view with regard to the question of election when he writes: 'What is the essential aspect of this mystery which is manifested in the universal appeal to salvation in Christ, if it is not the discovery of everything which Christ bore in himself from all eternity and on the basis of which God made all things through him and for him?' (cf. *ibid.*, p. 236 [where the Fr. is slightly abridged]). Compare H. de Lubac, *The Mystery of the Supernatural* (London, Dublin and Melbourne, 1967), esp. pp. 107ff.

7

The Spirit, the Spirit of Christ: Christomonism and the *Filioque*

I would like to begin this chapter by considering those Pauline texts that date from the years A.D. 54-57. Firstly, Gal 4:6-7: 'Because you are sons, God has sent the Spirit of his Son into our hearts, crying, "Abba! Father!" So through God you are no longer a slave, but a son and, if a son, then an heir'. The Apostle contrasts two principles of existence here. On the one hand, there is the law which makes us live according to the 'flesh'. On the other, there is faith, which makes us live from the Spirit and according to the Spirit. The Spirit carries out God's plan or purpose, which is to finish the task of (re-)making man in his image and making him a son.

Making someone in one's own image is, after all, begetting a child and Jesus was the Son in perfection (2 Cor 4:4; Col 1:15). We are united and assimilated to him by our faith, which is sealed in the baptism by which we receive the Spirit (Gal 3:26; 5:5). Through faith in Jesus Christ, we receive the object of the promise made to Abraham and his descendants. The latter form the Body of Christ and are 'sons in the Son', co-heirs with the Son and able to call God 'Father' with him.

I am impelled to quote at this point the parallel passage in Romans (8:15-17), which does not, however, speak of the 'Spirit of his Son': 'You have received the Spirit of sonship. When we cry, "Abba! Father!" it is the Spirit himself bearing witness with our spirit that we are children of God, and if children, then heirs, heirs of God and fellow heirs with Christ, provided we suffer with him in order that we may be glorified with him'.

The Spirit is therefore the Spirit of the Son because he has entered the Son's life as a son in a way that is effective in fulfilling the Promise. That functional reality clearly presupposes an ontological reality in order to provide a foundation for its existence and its truth, but Paul does not specify which one.

Next, Rom 8:9: 'But you are not in the flesh, you are in the Spirit, if the Spirit of God really dwells in you. Anyone who does not have the Spirit of Christ does not belong to him'. The Spirit is first and foremost the Spirit of

God and 'God' is the Father. But he is the Spirit of God, who works in Jesus Christ with our divine destiny in view. He 'anointed' Jesus and made him Christ through the Spirit. He also, through the Spirit, raised him from the dead, glorified him and made him Lord, that is, capable of giving the Spirit: 'If the Spirit of him who raised Jesus from the dead dwells in you, he who raised Christ Jesus from the dead will give life to your mortal bodies also through his Spirit which dwells in you' (8:11; cf. 1 Cor 15:42-45).

It is through that Spirit who was and is still active in Jesus Christ, then, that we have been made sons and live as sons (8:14-17). The Spirit is therefore the Spirit *of Christ* in the economy of grace through which the *Unigenitus* becomes *primogenitus in multis fratribus* — the 'first-born among many brethren' (see 8:29). We for our part 'reflecting the glory of the Lord, are being changed into his likeness from one degree of glory to another, for this comes from the Lord who is the Spirit' (2 Cor 3:18; cf. 1 Cor 15:49).

In Phil 1:19, the 'Spirit of Jesus Christ' is the principle of power and help enjoyed by Paul in his condition as a prisoner.

Peter speaks of the Spirit of Christ who was present in the prophets when they were asking to what time and circumstances the indications referred that had been given in advance by that Spirit regarding 'the sufferings of Christ and the subsequent glory' (1 Pet 1:11). Is the Spirit of God, who is traditionally connected with the activity of the prophets, involved here, and do the words 'of Christ' have in mind the Christological content of the prophets' proclamations? Or is Peter thinking of Christ's pre-existence intervening through his Spirit in those proclamations? Support for this hypothesis can possibly be found in the statement: 'He was (pre-)destined before the foundation of the world but was made manifest at the end of the times for your sake' (1:20). This would be an example of the texts cited by Pierre Benoît as pointing to Christ's pre-existence in a time and a mode of being that are different from those of the eternal Son.[1]

In Acts, the Spirit frequently intervenes to give guidance, even detailed guidance to the apostolate. In 16:7 he is called the 'Spirit of Jesus' and prevents Paul from going to Bithynia. It is Jesus or the Spirit who gives impetus to and at the same time restrains the apostolate. In many texts and even in the Gospel of Luke,[2] the same activity is attributed either to Christ or to the Spirit.

Let me now attempt to provide a conspectus of the whole. Despite the fact that different terms are used, these New Testament texts have a profound consistency. According to St Paul, the Son who was sent by God obtained for us the quality of (adopted) sons (Gal 4:5; Rom 8:3). John expresses this in terms of eternal life (Jn 3:14ff.). The end corresponds to this principle — it will be a sharing in the Father's inheritance (Gal 4:7; Rom 8:17, 21). This quality and life as sons is made active and effective in us by the Spirit. It is he who gives us life in Jesus Christ, and Christ who assimilates us to him (Rom 8:9-17). The Spirit makes us follow the way of Christ, that is, the way from the crucifixion of the flesh to glory. This is because he is the Spirit 'of Christ' in the same way as 'of God' (Rom 8:9).

Peter makes very similar affirmations, although the words that he uses are different. 'God the Father of our Lord Jesus Christ' has caused us to be 'born anew (*anagennaō*) through the resurrection of Jesus Christ...to an inheritance which is imperishable...in heaven' (1 Pet 1:3-4, 23). The means or the condition of this rebirth is faith in the 'living word of God' which is the 'seed' of that life (1:23) or the 'word of truth' (Jas 1:18, where the verb *apokueō*, to bring forth, give birth to, is used).

1 Jn 3:9 must be mentioned in this context: we are born of God (the verb here is *gennaō*) through his seed. The latter has been interpreted both as the word and as the Spirit and both have correspondences in John's Gospel. If the Word is 'received' by faith, what, then, is the 'power to become children of God' (Jn 1:12)? It must be the power that enables us to be born *anōthen*, 'from above' or 'anew', and that power is the Spirit (3:3-5). The same power to become a child of God is also explicitated in the following verse, which is read in the plural, although some evidence supports the singular: those 'who were born, not of blood nor of the will of the flesh nor of the will of man, but of God' (1:13). In the plural, this refers to us. In the singular, it refers to Jesus, who was born of Mary and the Holy Spirit. But it is the same mystery that is the object of God's election or purpose. It is always a question of the birth of the Word in us, the conception of a son of God in human flesh. When we are involved, the evangelist uses the word *tekna*, not *huioi* (see 1 Jn 3:1ff.), doubtless in order to emphasize the fact that God is the Father of Christ and our Father at different levels (see, for example, 'to my Father and to your Father' in Jn 20:17). The participation of which the Spirit is the agent on the basis of faith is, however, an assimilation to the Word who came into the world, but who was God, being eternally towards God (*pros Theon*, 1:1). That was, then, to be the way of life of the disciples — the Spirit was to make the Word present again in them, since 'whatever he hears he will speak'. He was also to glorify the Son, the Word, because he was to receive what was his and communicate it (16:13-14).

The texts that speak of the Spirit of the Son or of Christ are all concerned with the economy, God's plan working in the world. This also applies to all the statements in the New Testament on which Christian teaching about the Trinity is based. Even the statement in Jn 15:26 about 'the Spirit of truth who proceeds from the Father' forms part of a passage dealing with the economic coming or sending of that Spirit by Christ. It has been pointed out that the term 'Son' is only used frequently from the time of Jesus' public life onwards. This does not, however, lead me to favour a theology in the style of Piet

Schoonenberg. All Christian thinkers move from the economy to theology.[3] The Greek Fathers based their arguments for the divinity of the Son and the Spirit on this: they could not deify us if they were not themselves God. A similar approach is also presupposed in the Orthodox theology of the divine energies. The biblical evidence used to support this theology is, after all, found in texts that speak, for example, of the power, the light, the glory or the Face of God. These terms express manifestations of what God brings about for us. From this point, the next step is to affirm a reality *in God*.

The movement from the economy to theology, or rather the close connection between the two, is illustrated in the theology of the West by the profound doctrine of the 'divine missions', which is common property of that theology.[4] The Son, the Word, is sent into the world by the Father. The Breath, the Spirit, is sent by the Father and by the Son, Christ. This 'mission' postulates in the world and in men a new reality. That reality goes back to God's plan of grace, but its origin is no different from the divine Person who proceeds from the Father and, in the case of the Spirit, from the Father and from the Son.

Was the Son sent in our flesh? Through the incarnation, the Son proceeds from the Father in the flesh that he assumes. The eternal sending of the Word by the Father tends freely to end in the created nature assumed by the Word. The eternal word of the Father: 'Today I have begotten you' (Ps 2:7) takes on an entirely new meaning when the begetting of the Son ends in an actual created effect — the incarnation of Jesus in the womb of the Virgin Mary and then, made present and manifested once again, as we have already seen, in his baptism and finally in his resurrection and glorification. In that great and profound theology, the mission or sending of the Spirit by the Father and by the Son has its origin in the eternal mystery of the 'procession' of the Spirit from the Father conjointly with the Son.

This theology forms the basis of the idea that the Trinity of the economy is in fact identical with the Trinity of the eternal mystery. Karl Rahner, who calls this idea the *Grundaxiom* or 'fundamental axiom', adds *und umgekehrt* — 'and vice versa'. It is undeniably true that the economic Trinity is the eternal or immanent Trinity. Every theologian would accept this.[5] We have no other way of knowing the mystery of God apart from his revelation in the economy. But that has the depth and the concentration of a real self-communication. In the 'missions' of grace, the Word and the Spirit are given to us 'in usufruct'. This is what the Eastern Tradition calls 'deification'.

I would like to leave for the moment the criticism made by this Tradition of the Thomist explanation and its own doctrine of the 'energies', although I recognize its great importance. At this point, I would also prefer not to summarize the ways in which the economy of grace is communicated. This is because I have already done this in sufficient detail not only in my previous

books, but also in this one. I would rather review here and add to the criticism
that I have already provided of Karl Rahner's *umgekehrt* or 'vice versa', that
is, his idea of reciprocity.[6]

(1) If the mystery of the Tri-unity of God is revealed in the economy, is it
fully revealed? Jesus himself says: 'Who has seen me has seen the Father'. But
he also says: 'The Father is greater than I' and 'my Father and your Father,
my God and your God'. We Western Christians lack the systematic treatment
by the Eastern Church of the unknowability of God (the distinction between
God's communicable energies and his unknowable essence), but both in the
West and in the East, it is recognized that man cannot participate in the aseity
of God. Both the Latin and the Greek Church Fathers and theologians
insisted that they were not able to break through the difference between
'begetting' and 'procession' (the *ekporeusis* of the Spirit).[7]

(2) God's revelation and communication of himself takes place, in the
economy, in conditions of kenosis and the cross. The mode of reality of the
Trinitarian mystery in the eternity of God is always beyond what is
communicated to us and what is accessible to us.

The Orthodox Professor Megas Farentos has expressed almost exactly the
same reservations.[8] His article is well documented and the result is extremely
interesting. My only regret is that he is so negative and even aggressive in his
approach to Latin theology. He tries to force it to conclusions that are patently
unacceptable. That is altogether too much. And the mystery of the Holy
Triad is immeasurably beyond us all. I am, however, more especially
interested to know how justice is done in the Orthodox Tradition to the
statement that the Spirit is the Spirit *of the Son* because I have a very high
regard for Orthodox reflection about the mystery of the Trinity. For this
regard we have not only the riches of the Greek Fathers and the theologians,
but also formal studies by several contemporary authors.[9]

The writings of the Greek Fathers about this question seem to me to be
dominated by two factors:

(1) They have a very lively sense of the originality of the person. The
Latin and the Alexandrian Fathers are firmly attached to the consubstantiality
of the hypostases. No theologian would have anything to say against that, but
the statement that ' "person" signifies the irreducibility of man to his
nature'[10] suggests that Orthodox theologians are able to speak about the
hypostases without at the same time speaking about substance, and to use
different concepts. From the point of view of the hypostasis, the Spirit
proceeds only from the Father (*ekporeusis*) and a hypostasis can only come
from a hypostasis. From the point of view of the unity of essence or *ousia*, on
the other hand, the Spirit proceeds from the Father through the Son.

(2) Relationships between the Spirit and the Word are postulated in the
Greek Tradition, but other relationships apart from that of origin or

production are developed. There is a whole network of relationships between the divine Persons and a purely linear pattern of dependence is avoided, resulting in the Orthodox view of the permanently Trinitarian and reciprocal nature of those relationships.

One of the most frequent affirmations made by the Greek Fathers is that the Spirit was received by the Father in the Son and that he rests or dwells in the Son. This is clearly stated in a text of John Damascene.[11] He may possibly be referring here to Jn 1:32, but this text is about Christ and his baptism and has a different verb (*menō*). It is more likely that he has in mind Is 11:2, which has the same verb. All that he does in fact is to summarize the comments of the Fathers who have preceded him, namely Athanasius, Didymus and Gregory Nazianzen.[12] This 'resting' of the Spirit in the Son means that the latter is, in the words of Gregory Palamas, the 'treasurer of the Spirit', his personal abode.[13] This eternal relationship between the Son and the Spirit is the basis of the sending of the Spirit in us by the Son.

The Word and the Breath come simultaneously from the mouth of the Father in such a way that there is an order between them and that the Breath, the Spirit, is in the Son. He accompanies him and manifests his activity or energy. 'We have learned', John Damascene says, 'that the Spirit is he who accompanies (*sumparomartoun*) the Word and who reveals his operation (energy)'.[14] All the Greek authors stress repeatedly that the Spirit is always with the Son and that he accompanies him. They point to his presence in the economy of the incarnation, but affirm that presence in the eternal Triad.[15]

This remarkable text by Gregory Palamas is quoted by D. Staniloae (*op. cit.* below [note 9], p. 181): 'To accompany (*sumparomartein*) means to be together (*sunakolouthein*)... Thus the Spirit is not of the Son, but he is of the Father with the Son, insofar as the procession accompanies (*sunakolouthousēs*) the begetting, without temporal separation or distance'. The Spirit, then, completes the Holy Triad by being from the Father in the Son.

Gregory Nazianzen (Gregory the Theologian) says that God comes back into himself through the third Person, after his unity has become a duality.[16] Is that not what Dionysius, the Bishop of Rome, meant when he wrote to his namesake Dionysius of Alexandria in 262: 'It is necessary for the divine Word to be united with the God of the universe, for the Holy Spirit to abide and to dwell in God and for the divine Trinity to be recapitulated in and taken back to a single one, as to a peak, that is, the omnipotent God of the universe'.[17]

The Spirit, then, has the function of completing and therefore of confirming the unity in the diversity of the Persons. This function has, in my opinion, been expressd in a remarkably convincing way by a contemporary philosopher, who has succeeded in bringing together in this one function both the economy of the Spirit in the history of the Church — Tradition — and the intra-divine 'theology'. His words are worth quoting in this context:

'The same power of the Spirit to unite which keeps the Son in his origin in the Father and keeps Christ within the Father, also links our continuing human testimonies to the living Word, in which the divinity of God is expressed absolutely and is given infinitely'.[18]

This excellent text speaks of testimony or Tradition. But the function of the Spirit who, because he is resting in the Word, the Son, accompanies him, can also be applied to all the activities mentioned in the New Testament and above all to our own adoption as sons. It hardly needs to be said that this sonship is not purely juridical. It is something that makes us Christ's brothers. It is for us a rebirth, making us members of God's family.[19] It deifies us. As D. Staniloae says, 'the Spirit who makes his abode in us with the Son — and therefore in his quality as the Spirit of the Son — also makes us sons of the Father and thus deifies us'.

Although I cannot be sure of it, I hope that I have not misinterpreted the Orthodox understanding of the term 'Spirit of the Son' in what I have said above. In the Orthodox interpretation, a distinction is made between the economy, in which Christ gives the Spirit causally, and theology. At the intra-divine level of theology, the Spirit comes hypostatically from the Father alone, but has, with the Son, the Word, other relationships apart from that of causal production. This is sufficient to fulfil the letter of the New Testament texts, which express the economy.

The Latin Tradition, on the other hand, has stressed an ontological continuity between the economic relationship of the communicated Spirit and the eternal relationship between the Spirit and the Word. Like the Alexandrian Tradition, it has always been conscious of a process of substantial communication in the divine *ousia*, taking place through the processions from the Father, the Principle without a principle.

Theologians in the West have habitually turned to Scripture when dealing with the relationship between the Spirit and the Word. Thomas Aquinas, *Contra Gent*. IV, 24, cites, for example, Rom 8:9; Gal 4:6 and links these texts with Rom 8:29; Jn 15:26 and 16:14, combined with 16:15. He then sets about showing that an understanding of these texts at the purely economic level of the incarnate Word is not sufficient. In his *Contra Errores Graecorum* (a title which Thomas himself did not give to this treatise), he also cites other texts and supports them with evidence from the Greek Fathers (see II, c. 1).

Since Augustine, Latin thinking about the Trinity has been based on the distinction between what is expressed, in God, absolutely — that he is, for example, holy, wise, uncreated and omnipotent — and what is said in terms of relationship — that of the Father and the Son, for example. In the unity of substance, the Persons are distinguished by these relationships which are relationally opposed to each other. Anyone who is not allergic to the use of theological reasoning, in other words to reasoning in a demanding and

rigorous way while reflecting about the content of faith, will follow both
Anselm and Thomas in the kind of axiom that is dominant in their position,
namely that 'in God, all things are one when there is no opposition of
relationship of origin'.[20]

This is a fundamental principle. Both the Spirit and the Son proceed
equally from the Father. If there were no relationship of procession, which
could only go from the Son to the Spirit, between them, they could not be
distinguished as hypostases. It is therefore in a meaningful way that we speak
of the Spirit of the Son. The Councils of Lyons (1274) and Florence (1439)
both declared, following Augustine and Thomas Aquinas, that the Spirit
proceeds from the Father and from the Son — Filioque — as from one
principle. Orthodox Christians continue to object to this formula,
maintaining that, if this were the case, the Spirit would not proceed from a
hypostasis, but from what is common to those of the Father and the Son, that
is, from their common nature. Since that nature, however, is also common to
the Holy Spirit, the latter would also proceed from himself and that would be
absurd.

Thomas' reply to this objection is that the act of 'spiration' is a property of
the deity which is peculiar to the Persons of the Father and the Son, but which
may be common to both of them because it does not make them opposed to
one another. In that community of property, there is also an order, since the
Son receives it from the Father. The way in which Thomas received and
explained the formula 'from the Father through the Son' emphasizes the fact
that the Spirit proceeds from a single 'spirative' virtue, which is that of the
Father communicated to the Son with the essence (see *ST* Ia, q. 36, a. 3). As
H. F. Dondaine has pointed out, 'In other words, for the Son the spiration of
the Spirit is making him proceed from the Father' (vol. II [Paris, 1943], p.
326).

Jean-Miguel Garrigues has observed that, according to the Fourth Lateran
Council in 1215, the essence or substance was not held to produce, in other
words, it was not as such the principle of procession.[21] The conclusion that he
draws from this is that the only principle from which the Holy Spirit proceeds
is 'the Father himself, the source and origin of the entire Trinity'. This
formula, however, is ambiguous. On the one hand, it makes the Father the
only principle of spiration and thus results in a denial of the *Filioque*.
Alternatively, it may simply mean that the Son receives from the Father the
property of 'spiration', since he receives from him, with his hypostasis,
consubstantial divinity. That is Thomas' position.

Other formulae by Catholic authors better express the fact that it is not the
essence which is the principle of the procession of the Holy Spirit, but the
Persons. If it could be other than an image, St Bernard's formula would be
very satisfactory. With noble realism, he makes use of the image of the mutual

kiss. The Holy Spirit is the kiss which the Father and the Son give mutually to one another.[22] What proceeds from this — the kiss — is truly the action of two *persons*. It is really *duo Spiratores* rather than *unus Spirator, duo spirantes*, but it is not possible to go beyond the order of images.

Heribert Mühlen is more rigorous and takes as his point of departure the fact that active spiration is a personal act and, what is more, an act that is shared by the Father and the Son. It is, in other words, an act performed by two persons or a *Wir-Akt*. Passive spiration, which is the existence of the Spirit thus produced, is therefore the subsisting *Wir-Akt* and the Spirit is the *Wir in Person*, the 'We in person' or the relationship between 'Us' within the Trinity.[23]

I certainly like the beginning of Mühlen's theology. His treatment of active spiration as an act that is common to both the Father and the Son has the advantage of giving emphasis to the personal aspect, but his failure to postulate *duo Spiratores* presents us with a real problem. An even more unfortunate problem is present in his calling the Spirit *Wir in Person*, which surely applies to the Spirit what is common to both the Father and the Son as a personal attribute.

Orthodox Christians manage to avoid these difficult questions by insisting that the difference in the mode of production from the one monarchy of the Father creates a sufficient distinction between the hypostases of the Son and the Spirit. They also use two terms, 'begetting' and *ekporeusis* or 'coming out of', whereas the Latin Fathers employ the general word 'procession'. The former could even say that the Spirit 'proceeds' from the Son, using the verb *proïenai*, whereas, using the verb *ekporeuesthai*, he takes his hypostatic being from the one monarchy of the Father.

Is the difference in the mode of proceeding enought to make a distinction between the two hypostases? Thomas thought not, but Duns Scotus was much less sure of this. Had the matter really been proved? Begetting and *ekporeusis* are two different modes of production and are characterized by two different principles in the source of divinity, which Duns Scotus associated with nature and will.

Is what is required in the Latin construction of the mystery, then, also required by Christian faith in that mystery? It is true that this construction makes use of concepts that are beyond dispute — notably substance and relationship — but we lack any concept that can be satisfactorily applied within the Orthodox perspective. But do we really have to apply our confident Western rational logic to the intimate mystery of God?

There are also other difficulties. Do not two different processions of the Spirit presuppose, for example, two formalities in their common origin that are different in reality? It is said that the Spirit proceeds from the Father, but this is not from the Father as Father — it would make him a son or a brother of the Son, the Word. The scholastic theologians insisted that he proceeded from God, who is Father, or from the Father as *Auctor*, the absolute Principle. The Greeks, on the other hand, said that he proceeded from the Father as *Archē*, the first Principle, under the title of *Proboleus* (Gregory Nazianzen and John Damascene), the Father being the source of divinity before being (logically speaking) the pole of personal opposition. This is what is professed in the Creed: 'I believe in God (the source of divinity) the almighty Father'. As J.-M. Garrigues has remarked, it is true that the Creed connects the *ekporeusis* of the Spirit with the Father and not with the *Proboleus*. I would like to cite the passage in his book in which he discusses this question, because it represents an authentic attempt to bring together the two different dogmatic theologies that, I am convinced, express the same faith.

> If it is as Father that he (the Father) is the origin of the Spirit, this implies that he is so as the Father begetting the Son. The Father is therefore the source of the Spirit through and in the begetting of the Son which manifests him as Father. That is why the Spirit derives his origin from the Father in the Son whom he begets as the one principle of the whole Trinity. The procession of the Spirit *a Patre Filioque tamquam ab uno principio*, understood in this way, can therefore only be an explanation of the dogma of faith professed by the Council of 381 when it said that the Spirit had his *ekporeusis* from the Father and not, as might have been expected, from the *proboleus*. One of the Cappadocian Fathers, who played a leading theological part in that Council, Gregory of Nyssa, was also aware of the implication of the Son within the Father who was the cause, as Father, of the *ekporeusis* of the Spirit and said: 'Just as the Son is joined to the Father and receives his being from him without being later than him in his existence, so too does the Holy Spirit in his turn receive himself from the Son, who is contemplated before the hypostasis of the Spirit by virtue of the one Cause (the Father)' (*PG* 45, 464).[24]

J.-M. Garrigues has further developed an explanation that he first provided in 1972 (*Ist.*, 345-366) in the extremely interesting colloquium organized in October 1978 and May 1979 by the Faith and Order Commission of the World Council of Churches.[25] Three participants from different denominations of the Western Church as well as the authors of the final report that was approved by all the participants stressed the fact that the Spirit proceeds from the Father of the Son. The report stated 'While the Holy Spirit proceeds from the Father alone, his procession is nevertheless connected with the relationship within the Trinity between the Father and the Son, in virtue of which the Father acts *as Father*'.

J.-M. Garrigues has shown that this fundamental datum was differently conceptualized on the one hand by the Greek Fathers, the Cappadocians and John Damascene and, on the other, by the Latin Fathers from Tertullian onwards. Two explanations as to how a mutually recognized fact come to be differentiated in this way have led to what Garrigues has called two *theologoumena*, a term that was first used in this context by B. Bolotov in his remarkable and famous report of 1892.[26] The Greek and the Latin Fathers, Garrigues argues, each took a different problem as their point of departure.

The Cappadocian Fathers had to reply to Eunomius, who had applied to God the Neoplatonic idea of hierarchical emanations and subordinate participation. They were led to make an antinomic distinction in God between the divine essence and the hypostases. This made it possible for the Cypriot Patriarch Gregory and Gregory Palamas, for example, to speak in a differentiated way of the production of the third hypostasis and his participation in the common substance. The Latin Fathers from Tertullian onwards, on the other hand, preferred to stress the procession of the Persons in the divine essence.

In these conditions, Garrigues points out, the Greeks on the one hand saw in the (logically presupposed) begetting of the Son the negative condition of the fact that the *ekporeusis* of the Spirit, which was brought about exclusively by the Father, was not a second act of begetting. The Cappadocian and Byzantine theologoumenon is as follows: *ek monou tou Patros dia tou Huiou ekporeuomenon* ('the Spirit comes from the Father alone through the Son'). On the other hand, the Latin Fathers saw in the same begetting of the Son the positive condition (the non-principial cause) of the consubstantial procession of the Spirit in the communion of the Father and the Son. The Latin and Alexandrian theologoumenon is therefore expressed in Greek as: *ek tou Patros kai tou Huiou proïon* or in Latin as: *qui ex Patre Filioque procedit* ('the Spirit proceeds from the Father and the Son').

Union might possibly be achieved between East and West in a profession of the same central dogmatic core and a mutual recognition of two different, but not contradictory theologoumena. Garrigues, however, thinks that it may be possible to arrive at a single formula. The first step towards this would be to improve the vocabulary used. In the Creed, the word *ekporeuomenon* should not be translated by *qui procedit*, but by 'who betakes himself out of the Father' or more simply by 'who goes out of the Father'. *Procedere*, on the other hand, means to go forward, making room for that from which one is removing oneself. This is rendered in Greek by *prochōrein*. This improved vocabulary would, in Garrigues' opinion, enable certain nuances unfortunately lacking in the translation of *ekporeuesthai* by *procedere* to be included in the formula. The final formula suggested by Garrigues as ecumenically possible is as follows: 'The Holy Spirit, coming out of the Father alone, who begets the one Son, proceeds from the two'. This is expressed in Greek as: *ek monou tou Patros ton Monogenē gennōntos ekporeuomenon kai ap'amphoin prochōron* and in Latin as: *Ex unico Patre unicum Filium generante se exportans, ab utroque procedit.*

The word *exportans* lacks elegance and it might be better to go back to the suggestion made by M. J. Scheeben in the nineteenth century and translate *ekporeuesthai*, as he did, by *emitti* or *emanere* and *proïenai* by *procedere*. For his formula, however, Garrigues can certainly claim the support of Maximus the Confessor, the Greek theologian whose work is shared by both sides, in his famous letter to Marinus, and of both Gregory of Cyprus and Gregory Palamas.

Dumitru Staniloae's criticism of Garrigues' suggestions has, however, drawn my attention both to the difficulty of achieving agreement at the level of formulae and to the ease with which our different positions can be misunderstood.[27] It may well be presumptuous and even futile to try to achieve reunion between the two Traditions by means of a single formula. It would perhaps be better to have full explanations on both sides with serious attempts at mutual understanding, followed by a recognition of the possibility of the co-existence of the two Traditions in professing and living the same faith, on condition that both adhered to the Creed formulated by the First Council of Constantinople in 381 as a normative text.

This is what was made manifest and proclaimed during the celebrations in Rome and Istanbul at Whitsun 1981. On the Catholic side, this was preceded by and announced in a letter written by Pope John Paul II, dated 25 March 1981 and entitled *A Concilio Constantinopolitano*,[28] in which the Pope said: 'The teaching of the First Council of Constantinople still is and always will be the expression of the one common faith of the Church and the whole of Christianity'. He repeated this statement in his homily at Pentecost and in the letter that he wrote to the Oecumenical Patriarch Dimitrios I.[29] The letter announcing the celebration also described the Creed of 381 as normative and irrevocable. This Creed was cited by the Pope significantly without the interpolation of the *Filioque*.

In his homily during the celebration itself, the Pope also described the faith expressed in the Creed of the First Council of Constantinople as something that 'we would like to profess, teaching it in 1981 with the purity and the force with which that venerable Council professed it and had it professed sixteen centuries ago'. He proclaimed the text of 381, then, as absolutely normative and this also means that the *Filioque* has to be understood in conformity with it. This is important with regard to the objective content of Christian teaching. It is also important from the formal point of view of theological criteriology. What the Pope was professing was that the norm for the expression of the Church's faith was the Oecumenical Council, in this case, that of 381, and he was himself submitting to that norm.

It has often been said that the *Filioque* has led in Western Christianity to very decisive consequences in the sphere of anthropology, in the sacraments and above all in ecclesiology. I could easily write a book about this question, but will do no more here than simply provide a broad outline, mentioning some of the studies in which I have already dealt with it and those to which I have referred.

Vladimir Lossky, who has played a remarkably important part in throwing light on and bringing up to date the great Tradition of the Eastern Orthodox Church, is the scholar who has been mainly responsible for tracing the differences between Roman Catholicism and the Orthodox Church back to the consequences of the *Filioque*. I have made use here of the summary provided by André de Halleux and based on Lossky's work:[30]

> The Spirit is here reduced to the function of a link between the two other Persons and one-sidedly subordinated to the Son in his very existence in contempt of the genuine perichoresis. He thereby loses, together with his hypostatic independence, the personal fullness of his economic activity. The latter is henceforth seen as a simple means of serving the economy of the Word, both at the level of the Church and at that of the person. The goal of the Christian way of life therefore becomes the *imitatio Christi*, no longer a deification by the Holy Spirit. The people of God are subjected to the body of Christ, the charism is made subordinate to the institution, inner freedom to imposed authority, prophetism to juridicism, mysticism to scholasticism, the laity to the clery, the universal priesthood to the ministerial hierarchy, and finally the college of bishops to the primacy of the Pope. Creative and renewing source as he is, the Spirit was nevertheless expropriated by the Catholic Church, which made that Spirit the supreme guardian of the dispensation set up by Christ in favour of his Vicar. The Orthodox Church, on the other hand, has preserved the mutual subordination and the fertile tension between the economy of the incarnation and that of Pentecost.

Professor Nikos Nissiotis has several times accused the Roman Catholic Church, in a less polemical tone than Lossky, but equally radically, of 'Christomonism'.[31] Everything, he claims, is seen one-sidedly as referring to Christ. The Spirit is merely added to a Church, its ministries and its sacraments, all of which are already constituted. The Spirit simply carries out a function of Christ.

This is a criticism that was made by almost all observers at the Council throughout the whole of Vatican II. We who participated in the Council's work tried to take this criticism into account, all the more so because we were ourselves elaborating a pneumatology at the time. Paul VI, who spoke so well and so much about the Holy Spirit,[32] pointed out on one occasion at least that

the Spirit was mentioned 258 times in the conciliar documents.[33] This is in
itself remarkable, but it does not in itself constitute a pneumatology.[34] It is
quite unjust to claim that *Lumen Gentium* had no more than a 'sprinkling' of
the Holy Spirit,[35] but there have been so many criticisms of the relative
absence of the Spirit from this document, from *Dei Verbum* and from other
conciliar texts that I am bound to devote my attention to this question.[36] In the
remaining pages of this chapter, then, I shall look closely at this criticism of
'Christomonism' and the absence of pneumatology in the whole of the
Western Catholic tradition as well as in the teaching of Vatican II and since
the Council.

I have already studied certain aspects of this question and in particular
those relating to the theology of the Eucharist, that of grace, that of the
Mystical Body,[37] and finally ecclesiology.[38] The scholastic theologians and
especially Thomas Aquinas attributed (or appropriated) to the Holy Spirit the
virtue of the sacraments, but they also subjected them to the impulse and the
grace of Christ.[39] We can hardly criticize them for doing this, but the result
has been that the theologians of the Western Church are accused of
'Christomonism' in precisely that place where they attribute the same
function to the Holy Spirit as the Orthodox theologians.[40]

All the same, there is certainly some justification for their criticism. The
profound and very fine view of the liturgy provided by Pius XII in *Mediator
Dei* (20 November 1947) is, for example, essentially Christological.[41] Then
there is the question of the Church. Its structures and its life were described
with a fine Trinitarian balance in the great classical period from the third to
the fourth centuries. From the end of the apostolic period onwards, however,
there has been a tendency to lose sight of the Pauline teaching that the Holy
Spirit is, through his gifts, present and active in all believers.

The idea that unity required submission to the same leader, moreover, soon
made its appearance. The pattern of one God, one bishop and one faith
unanimously professed, can already be seen in the writings of Ignatius of
Antioch. The context within which this profile developed is that of the idea of
the unity of God. This came partly from the Old Testament. It also came to
some extent from the Hellenistic and Stoic philosophy by which the early
Church was surrounded and which saw in the unity of the cosmos a reflection
and a consequence of the unity of God.[42]

The pattern according to which there could not be *unum corpus*, one Body,
without *unum caput*, one Head, finally came to dominate the Western
Church's ecclesiological thinking. This led to only a very partial realization in
the Church of such features as local councils and the Consistory of Cardinals
at Rome, the purely temporary or momentary appearance of conciliarism and
Gallicanism and the later emergence of the principle of the complementarity
of collegiality or co-responsibility as proclaimed in the famous Canon 34 of

the Apostles.[43] To this can also be added the idea that the Church is above all 'universal' and that the *unum caput* is the Pope, the 'vicar of Christ'. All this is very well known.

Until relatively recently, this view of the Church was supported by theologians, who, with very few exceptions (Möhler, Newman and others), regarded the activity of the Holy Spirit as divided between two spheres. On the one hand, the Spirit was seen as having an ecclesiological function and therefore as guaranteeing the institution of the Church and primarily that of the *magisterium*. On the other hand, he was seen as active in the inner life of believers. This, however rich it might be, did not, of course, constitute a pneumatology. Manning is, in my opinion, a very representative figure in this pattern of ecclesiology.

The movement of ideas that prepared the way for Vatican II, then the Council itself and finally the continuing developments in theology since the Council all point to the fact that the one-sidedness of the past has been and is still being corrected. The way is now open for a real pneumatology to be developed in the Church. I must have had a premonition of what would have to be done when I wanted the first volume in my series 'Unam Sanctam' to be a new translation into French of Möhler's *Die Einheit in der Kirche*, entitled *L'unité dans l'Eglise ou le principe du Catholicisme d'après l'esprit des Pères de trois premiers siècles*.[44] My reason was that I was reacting against a too juridical and too purely Christological ecclesiology. Möhler provided an antidote to this, although his own reaction was very one-sidedly in favour of the Holy Spirit, who appears in his work as creating the Church as his corporification.[45] He himself later tried to redress the balance in his thinking by making it more Christological.[46]

I have outlined elsewhere the place given to the Holy Spirit by the Second Vatican Council.[47] It is more important here to mention the developments that have led me to try to elaborate a full ecclesiological pneumatology since the Council.[48] In this task, I have derived great benefit from the encouragement given by my Orthodox friends and from my reading of the Church Fathers.

Everything depends on a recognition of the fact that the Church is constituted by and lives, in continuity from its origins, from the gifts distributed by the Lord and the Spirit for the building up of the Body of Christ (see 1 Cor 12:4-30). All these gifts contribute something to that task. The presbyterate and the episcopate are, moreover, no longer seen as having an exclusively direct and vertical relationship with Christ. They are now seen within the same framework and as defined by their ordination, which forms their link with the apostolic institution. That ordination itself is, however, not without a link with the community of believers. In the first place, it is made for that community and, in the second, believers themselves also play a part in it, by choosing their ministers, by the witness that they bear in it and by their union with it in the epiclesis of ordination, in which the Spirit is invoked. A bishop is normally consecrated, according to the Council of Nicaea, by at least three of his fellow-bishops. These fellow-bishops bear witness to the part played by other churches, manifest the apostolicity of the faith of the new bishop who has been elected and testify to the catholicity of the communion of churches.

Each local church possesses the gifts of evangelical faith and grace, but it is not alone in having received them. The fullness of the gifts of the Spirit only exists within the communion of the churches. The Spirit, who is the same in all the churches, is the guarantee both of that communion and of the diversity of the gifts. This life in communion calls for various interchanges between the churches of the kind that were common in the ancient world and for different forms of what might be called the synodical life of the Church — commissions, conferences of bishops, synods and councils. This is well illustrated in Canon 34 of the Apostles, to which I have already referred above:

> The bishops of every nation should know which of them is the first and whom they regard as their head (*hōs kephalēn*). They should do nothing without his consent, even if it is necessary for each one to deal with the affairs of his own diocese and the territories that form part of it. But he too (that is, the one who is the first) should do nothing without the consent (*gnōmē*) of all the others. In that way, concord (*homonoia*) will prevail and God will be glorified by the Son in the Holy Spirit.[49]

What is suggested in this excellent text is a Trinitarian model for the Church and a structure for communion that incorporates synodality and what might be termed cephality. Within a structure of this type, unity is sought, not in submission to the authority of a single leader, but in reciprocal relationships and in consensus. A Catholic ecclesiology would be more concerned with that form of authority. The importance attached in the Catholic Church to the function of the bishop of Rome is well known, but this has to be assessed much more precisely.[50] A great deal of historical, theological and juridical work has still to be done if we are to achieve an entirely valid synthesis.

There is no need to stress pneumatology in the liturgy. If the Roman Catholic and Eastern Orthodox members of the International Commission were able to give unanimous approval on 6 July 1982 to the text on the 'mystery of the Church and the Eucharist in the light of the mystery of the Holy Trinity',[51] this must surely be a sign that there are, at that level at least, only two sections of the one Church. What is more, the one place where Christology and pneumatology are united is undoubtedly the liturgy. In its contents, those who perform it and its whole context, in its combination of word and activity, spirit and form and finally as a celebration on the part of Christ as the great High Priest and the coming of the Holy Spirit into our hearts, it is instituted by Christ and constitutes an event of grace.

To return to the question of the decisive and universal impact of the *Filioque*, I would agree that the criticism of 'Christomonism' in Western Catholicism is to some extent right, but I have, I think, shown that this is being corrected. At the same time, it has to be frankly admitted that several studies seem to me to have been artificially reconstructed and to contain fundamentally only what the author likes or dislikes.[52] We should not, surely, simply make a list of what we like and call it pneumatology and then of what we dislike and call it Roman Catholic juridicism! The same procedure could be applied to the Orthodox Church — we could reconstruct a number of correct or disputed texts and conclude that the Orthodox rejection of the *Filioque* has produced the effects which Professor Megàs Farentos challenges in the work of Karl Barth and Helmut Thielicke.[53] We cannot reject *a priori* the idea that a one-sided approach may slide imperceptibly into the development of a pneumatology. Georges Dejaifve, who knows and loves the Orthodox Church, has warned Orthodox theologians of the danger of attributing an autonomy to the Holy Spirit. We should therefore cease to quarrel in this way.

I am convinced that the differences between the two traditions are the result of two different approaches and two different constructions of the relationships between nature and what I would call the supernatural. There is also the problem of different anthropological understandings of the image and likeness of God. Finally, the theologies of the East and the West have different philosophical orientations — towards Plato or towards Aristotle, and thus either towards participation or towards causality. With some hesitation, because of their limitations, I would suggest that some of my youthful articles may still be worth reading in this context.[54]

Notes

1 E. G. Selwyn, *The First Epistle of Peter* (London, 1958), p. 136, note, cites Melito, who, in his homily on the Passion, attributes the Old Testament miracles to Christ.

2 See, for example, Luke (21:12-15), who attributes to Christ the help that Matthew (10:18-20) and Mark (13:9-11) attribute to the Spirit.

3 A. M. Dubarle, 'Les fondements bibliques du "Filioque" ', *ReC*, 4. Ser. 2 (1950), 229-244, bases this approach on New Testament evidence.

4 For Thomas Aquinas, see *In I Sent*. d. 14 to 16; *ST* Ia, q. 43. See also Dom

Lucien Chambat, *Présence et union, Les missions des Personnes de la Sainte Trinité selon saint Thomas d'Aquin* (Abbaye de Saint-Wandrille, 1945).

5 This has been affirmed more strongly by Karl Barth than by anyone else. According to Professor Megas Farentos, 'Bemerkungen zur Trinitäts- und Geisteslehre des Glaubensbekenntnisses von Nizäa-Konstantinopel', *Le IIe Concile oecuménique. Signification et actualité pour le monde chrétien d'aujourd'hui* (*Etudes théologiques* 2; Chambésy, 1982), p. 247, 'The fundamental correctness of this statement is not disputed by Orthodox theology . . .'. Gregory of Nyssa goes so far as to affirm that the individual way in which each Person assumes the energy that is common to their manifestation in the part that they play in the economy is not different from their mode of existence in the eternity of the deity.

6 Yves Congar, *I Believe in the Holy Spirit* III (London and New York, 1983), pp. 13-18.

7 The Greek Fathers: references in *I Believe in the Holy Spirit, op. cit.*, p. 45 note 41. The Latin Fathers: Augustine, *Contra Maxim*. II, 14, 1; Anselm, *Mon*. 61, 64 and 65.

8 M. Farentos, 'Bemerkungen . . .', *op. cit.*, pp. 235-257, especially pp. 244f.

9 I would mention especially in the volume cited below (note 25), pp. 174-186, the concentrated study by Professor Dumitru Staniloae, 'The Procession of the Holy Spirit from the Father and his Relation to the Son, as the Basis of our Deification and Adoption'.

10 These words were written by V. Lossky, *In the Image and Likeness of God* (London and Oxford, 1975), p. 120.

11 John Damascene, *De fide orthod*. I, 8 and 13 (*PG* 94, 821 and 857). See also the long scholarly note by J. Grégoire, 'La relation éternelle de l'Esprit au Fils d'après les écrits de Jean de Damas', *RHE* 64 (1969), 703-755, especially 728f., note 2.

12 See Athanasius, *Ad Ser*. I, 14 (*PG* 26, 565B; *SC* 15, p. 107); Didymus the Blind, *De Trin*. I, 31 (*PG* 39, 425A; with *para*). Thomas Aquinas deals with this idea in an objection made to the *Filioque*: *ST* Ia, q. 36, a. 2, ad 4. The reference is to the *Martyrium Andreae* (*Ep. pres. et diac. Achaiae*), Prol. (*PG* 2, 1217). See also M. Bonnet, *Acta Apostolorum Apocryph*. II, 1 (1898), p. 2.

13 Gregory Palamas, *Works* (in Greek), ed. P. Christou, I (Thessalonika, 1962), p. 56. Cited by D. Staniloae, p. 180.

14 John Damascene, *De fide orthod*. I, 7 (*PG* 94, 805). Cited by D. Staniloae, p. 181, who notes that the term is borrowed almost literally from Gregory of Nyssa (*PG* 45, 17). The word *sumparomartein* is also used by Gregory Nazianzen, for example, in his *Orat*. 42, 11.

15 See T. de Régnon, *Etudes sur la Sainte Trinité* IV (Paris, 1898), pp. 141f. and 148 (a remarkable text by Cyril of Alexandria).

16 Gregory Nazianzen, *Orat. de Filio* (*PG* 36, 76); *Orat. de pace* (*PG* 35, 1160).

17 Preserved by Athanasius, *De decret. Nicenae Synodi*, c. 26 (*DS* 112).

18 Claude Bruaire, 'Le Dieu de l'histoire', *Communio* IV (November-December 1979), p. 7.

19 Jn 1:12-13; 1 Jn 3:1-2, 10; 5:1, 4, 18; Tit 3:7; 1 Pet 1:23, etc.

20 In the literal form (*In Deo omnia sunt unum ubi non obviat relationis oppositio*), the axiom is not found in Anselm, although it is found as far as the sense is concerned. See *De proc. spir. sanct.* 1: S. Schmitt (ed.), *Opera* II (Rome, 1940), p. 180, l. 27; p. 181, l. 2-4; p. 183, l. 3. This is a very important theological principle, not a dogmatic formula. See my *I Believe in the Holy Spirit, op. cit.* (note 6), III, pp. 98 and 102 note 9.

21 Fourth Lateran Council, c. 2 (*DS* 804). See also J.-M. Garrigues, *L'Esprit qui dit 'Père' et le problème du Filioque* (Paris, 1982), pp. 111-112.

22 Bernard, *In Cant. sermo* 8, 2f. (*PL* 183, 811f.). See also J. Leclercq, *Le mariage vu par les moines au XIIe siècle* (Paris, 1983), pp. 114ff.

23 H. Mühlen, *Der Heilige Geist als Person. In der Trinität, bei der Inkarnation und in der Gnadenbund. Ich–Du–Wir* (*MBTh* 26; Münster, 3rd ed., 1969), p. 157.

24 J.-M. Garrigues, *op. cit.* (note 21), p. 118.

25 L. Vischer (ed.), *Spirit of God, Spirit of Christ: Ecumenical Reflections on the Filioque Controversy* (Faith and Order Paper no. 103; London, 1981), pp. 149-163 (Garrigues), 14 (statement).

26 German text: *RITh* 6 (1898), 681-712: Fr. trans.: *Ist.* 17 (1972), 261-289. As B. Bobrinskoy has correctly pointed out (*op. cit.* [note 25], p. 135 note 5), Bolotov did not accord to the *Filioque*, the status and dignity of a theologoumenon. In my view, he was wrong, since the doctrine of the *Filioque* would seem to satisfy the conditions that he states are required for a theologoumenon.

27 It astonishes me that such a distinguished scholar as Fr Staniloae should go so far as to say that the Spirit can only be the Spirit of the Son if he does not proceed from the Son. His words are: 'If the Spirit also comes from the Son, he would no more be the Spirit of the Son, but would be exclusively the Spirit of the Father. Consequently the *filioque* is opposed to our adoption as sons by the Spirit of the Son' (*op. cit.* [note 9], pp. 176-177). He also says further on: 'In the East, it is not denied that at the origin of the sending of the Spirit by the Son there is a special eternal relationship between the Son and the Spirit, just as there is such an eternal relationship between the Father and the Son at the origin of the sending of the Son into the world. In the West, on the other hand, one avoids drawing from the eternal relation of the Spirit to the Son, the conclusion that the Spirit is sent to men for a work which consists essentially in the deification and adoption of man' (p. 178). This is not a true interpretation of our positions!

28 Dimitrios I also wrote an encyclical especially for the centenary of the Council of 381. I have studied this letter with interest, but regret to find one sentence in it: 'That is why the addition of the *Filioque* in the matter of the eternal procession of the Holy Spirit from the Father, that is, not from one single source of divinity, but from two ... has to be rejected'. See no. 14 of the encyclical *Episkepsis*, no. 254 (15 June 1981), 11; *Irén.* 54 (1981), 230. This is an imprecise statement and an unjust accusation. For the Latin terms for the 'monarchy' of the Father, see my *I Believe in the Holy Spirit, op. cit.* (note 6), III, pp. 134-140. The formula *tanquam ab uno Principio*, which contradicts the preceding formula, is also criticized.

29   John Paul II, letter *A Concilio CPno*; homily preached at Pentecost; and letter to
      Dimitrios I; *DC* 1811 (5 July 1981), pp. 617-620 and 622-623.

30   André de Halleux, *RThL* 6 (1975), 13-44, following V. Lossky, *The Mystical
      Theology of the Eastern Church* (London, 1957), pp. 156-157, 164, 166-167,
      184-185, 192-193, 243-244. See also O. Clément, 'Vladimir Lossky, un
      théologien de la personne et du Saint-Esprit', *Messager de l'exarchat du patriarche
      russe en Europe occidentale* 8 (1959), pp. 137-206, especially pp. 201-204.
      References to other authors will be found in my essay cited below (note 31), p. 58
      note 72.

31   See note 2 in my essay 'Pneumatologie ou "Christomonisme" dans la tradition
      latine?', *Ecclesia a Spiritu Sancto edocta. Mélanges Gérard Philips (BEThL
      XXVII; Gembloux, 1970), pp. 42-63; previously published in *EThL* 45 (1969),
      394-416. I could, if it were not pointless to do so, add a few more references now
      to Nissiotis and several others.

32   See Daniel-Ange, *Paul VI. Un regard prophétique*, 2: *L'éternelle Pentecôte* (Paris
      and Fribourg, 1981).

33   Paul VI, audience held on 23 May 1973: see *DC* 1634 (17 June 1973), p. 552; see
      also *DC* 1635, p. 601.

34   O. Clément observed this: 'Quelques remarques d'un Orthodoxe sur la
      constitution "De Ecclesia" ', *Oec.* (1966), 97-116.

35   This expression was used by G. Westphal, *Vie et foi du Protestant* (Paris, 1966),
      p. 134.

36   Apart from N. Nissiotis and O. Clément, see the following for the Protestant
      point of view: V. Vajta, 'La refonte de la liturgie au concile oecuménique de
      Vatican II', G. A. Lindbeck (ed.), *Le dialogue est ouvert* (Neuchâtel, 1967), I, pp.
      110-111; H. Roux, 'Le décret sur l'activité missionaire de l'Eglise', *Vatican II.
      Points de vue de théologiens protestants (Unam Sanctam* 64; Paris, 1967), pp.
      112-114; G. G. Blum, *Offenbarung und Überlieferung. Die dogmatische
      Konstitution Dei Verbum des II. Vatikanums* (Göttingen, 1971), pp. 189-206.

37   In my essay, *op. cit.* (note 31).

38   In my *I Believe in the Holy Spirit, op. cit.* (note 6), I, pp. 151-157 and 163.

39   See, for example, Thomas Aquinas, *ST* IIIa, q. 8, a. 1, ad 1; q. 63, a. 3, obj. 1 and
      ad 1; q. 65, a. 4; q. 72, a. 1, ad 1.

40   This is so in the case of the theme studied by N. Nissiotis, 'Der
      pneumatologische Ansatz und die liturgische Verwirklichung des
      neutestamentlichen *nun*', *Oikonomia. Heilsgeschichte als Thema der Theologie.
      Festgabe O. Cullmann* (Hamburg and Bergstadt, 1967), pp. 302-309.

41   See *DS* 3840; *AAS* 39 (1947), 528.

42   I follow H. Mühlen, *Morgen wird Einheit sein* (Paderborn, 1974), pp. 138ff.,
      here. For the reference to Ignatius of Antioch, see pp. 144f.

43   The idea of *unum corpus (quia) unum caput* could be illustrated by hundreds of
      texts, going back to the most classical. See, for example, Thomas Aquinas,
      Contra Gent. IV, 76; Boniface VIII, Bull *Unam Sanctam* (18 November 1302; *DS*
      872). See also the references given in *L'Episcopat et l'Eglise universelle (Unam
      Sanctam* 39; Paris, 1962), p. 245 note 2. For the period following Vatican I, see
      my *I Believe in the Holy Spirit, op. cit.*, I, pp. 160-161.

44 It was only because I had to commission a new translation that I published Möhler's classical work as the second volume (1938) rather than as the first in the series.

45 Hence the surprising judgement of the Orthodox theologian Georges Florovsky in *Put'* (1927), 128ff., cited by S. Tyszkiewicz, *L'Eglise est une. Hommage à Möhler* (Paris, 1939), p. 279: 'Möhler's teaching has the defect that characterizes most of Western theology — it lacks a Christological foundation. Möhler has made very little use of the definition of the Church provided by the Apostle: the Body of Christ. It is possible to say that in the Church the Holy Spirit creates his own Body and not the Body of Christ and that the Body conceals the Head, the King, the Pontiff and the Prophet. This "dogmatic break" weakens the significance of his confession of faith in the *sobornost'*.

46 There are many early studies. More recently, J. Rosato has studied this question in 'Between Christocentrism and Pneumatocentrism. An Interpretation of J. A. Möhler's Ecclesiology', *HeyJ* (1978), 46-70.

47 Y. Congar, *I Believe in the Holy Spirit, op. cit.*, I, pp. 167-172; *idem*, 'Les implications christologiques et pneumatologiques de l'ecclésiologie de Vatican II', G. Alberigo (ed.), *Les Eglises après Vatican II. Dynamisme et prospective. Actes du Colloque international de Bologne, 1980 (ThH* 61; Paris, 1981), pp. 117-138.

48 See H. Legrand, 'Le développement d'Eglises-sujets à la suite de Vatican II. Fondements théologiques et réflexions institutionelles', *Les Eglises après Vatican II, op. cit.*, pp. 149-184. See also my *I Believe in the Holy Spirit, op. cit.*, II; 'Une pneumatologie ecclésiologique', *Initiation à la pratique de la théologie*, II: *Dogmatique* I (Paris, 1982), pp. 483-516.

49 Ed. F. X. Funk (1905), I, pp. 572-574; Fr. trans. by Pierre Duprey, 'La structure synodale de l'Eglise dans la tradition orientale', *POC* 20 (1970), 124.

50 See J. M. R. Tillard, *The Bishop of Rome* (London and Wilmington, Del., 1983). In my bulletins in the *RSPhTh*, I have followed the progress of serious historical studies concerned with the councils and the papacy.

51 The text will be found in *Irén.* 55 (1982), 350-362.

52 See, for example, N. Nissiotis, 'La pneumatologie ecclésiologique au service de l'unité de l'Eglise', *Ist.* (1967), 323-340; W. Hryniewicz, 'Der pneumatologische Aspekt der Kirche aus orthodoxer Sicht', *Cath.* 31 (1977), 122-150.

53 M. Farentos, *op. cit.* (note 5), pp. 245 and 250f.

54 Y. Congar, 'Deification in the Spiritual Tradition of the East' (Fr. orig. 1935), *Dialogue between Christians* (London and New York, 1966), pp. 217-231; *idem*, 'The Human Person and Human Liberty in Oriental Anthropology' (Fr. orig. 1952), *ibid.*, pp. 232-245.

8

The Holy Spirit in the cosmos

The Spirit is interiority and freedom. He is given 'in our hearts'. We call on him as we call on a gentle and beloved guest in our souls — *dulcis hospes animae*. We also call on him, however, as the creator — *Veni, creator Spiritus*. In the liturgy, we see him in the perspective of our inner, spiritual life.

The creative aspect of the Spirit is revealed in the familiar text of Genesis describing the act of creation: 'the Spirit of God was moving over the face of the waters' (1:3). This image is that of a bird whose time of brooding is over and whose clutch has come into existence. The cosmic theme of the Spirit as creator has hardly been developed at all in Catholic theology. Reviewing the German translation of my *I Believe in the Holy Spirit*, Jürgen Moltmann made precisely that comment — that there was no development of the cosmic role of the Spirit.[1] I have treated that as an invitation to devote this final chapter to what I hope my readers will allow me to call, in my own jargon, a few elements of pneumatological anthropology (although I would point out that the same jargon is also used by Nikos Nissiotis) and — another piece of theological jargon — pneumatological cosmism. Since jargon already abounds in this paragraph, let me add another term. These two spheres of theology depend on a third, pneumatological Christology.

This third sphere could equally well be called Christological pneumatology, since the Spirit is relative to Christ. In anthropological terms, it is a matter of making sons of God out of fleshly men, that is, men 'born of blood' and 'the will of the flesh' (Jn 1:13), men who are sinful. We have to be born or, in the words of St Bonaventure, created a second time.[2] Luther was conscious of the role of the Spirit as creator in his restitution and consolation of man who was lost and committed to the mortal trial of sin,[3] seeing the work of the Spirit as making Christ present and living in the word, in man through faith (*fides Christi*), and in the sacrament.

It is, then, the Spirit who gives life and enables us to act as adopted sons of God (Gal 4:6; Rom 8:13-16). He is able to achieve that because he is the Spirit *of the Son* and the one who introduced the Son into this world in the womb of the Virgin Mary. He enables us to conform to the filial life of Jesus, that life which Jesus led, in a humanity that is similar to our own, as a perfect human expression of orientation towards the Father (*pros ton Patera*, 1 Jn 1:2; Jn 1:1-2). Ignatius of Antioch had this in mind when he wrote: 'There is no longer any fire of love for matter in me now. All that is left is living water, murmuring in me and saying: "Come to the Father" '.[4]

This life as a child of God, coming 'from above' (Jn 3:3), can 'well up to eternal life' (4:14). As children of God, we are God's heirs and co-heirs with the Son (Gal 4:7; Rom 8:17). In the third article of the Creed, that which speaks of the Holy Spirit, we confess one baptism for the remission of sins, resurrection from the dead and eternal life to come.

It is possible for us to see, then, that there is no break, but on the contrary a close and intimate bond between the part played by the Spirit in our hearts and his cosmic role. This bond is made explicit in the text of Rom 8:19-25 and even as far as verse 30, a text I never tire of rereading. It comes immediately after the text to which I have just referred and which calls us 'fellow heirs with Christ, provided we suffer with him in order that we may also be glorified with him' (Rom 8:17). Omitting the intervening verse, we read:

> For the creation waits with eager longing for the revealing of the sons of God; for the creation was subject to futility, not of its own will, but by the will of him who subjected it in hope, because the creation itself will be set free from its bondage to decay and obtain the glorious liberty of the children of God. We know that the whole creation has been groaning in travail together until now; and not only creation, but we ourselves, who have the first fruits of the Spirit, groan inwardly as we wait for adoption as sons, the redemption of our bodies. For in this hope we were saved.

This passage does not deal with the first moment of creation, when God called beings into life. The Spirit was active then by virtue of his consubstantiality and the perichoresis of the divine Persons.[5] Paul is concerned here with the continuation and the end of the history of salvation. That history is inseparably Christological and pneumatological. It is filled with Christ and the Spirit. The absolute fullness that is in Christ is made present here and now and fulfilled by the Spirit in our history. This is accomplished by the Spirit because he first filled Christ and found in him total openness to the gift of God, the Promise made to our fathers.[6] What I have written above in Chapter 6 about pneumatological Christology and our election, which includes creation and salvation to the point of being 'glorified' (Rom 8:30) applies here.

We are sons, then. We are sons through the Spirit of Christ, whom we have received as earnest-money, that is, as the beginning of the first gift of the promised inheritance. This sets us firmly on the way to freedom. We do not yet enjoy the condition of being sons, which is glory and freedom. In that respect, we are like Christ, who was entirely Son. He was subjected to a condition of kenosis and obedience to the point of dying on a cross before he was able to enter, in his very humanity, into the condition of lordship that was appropriate to the Son of God.

Paul speaks of 'creation' in the sense of a universality of beings who are not God. Nowadays, our vision of that universe is immensely greater and we are also better able to envisage its development. We see it as one and as made of the same matter and the same chemical substances. We are conscious of its being totally embraced within a history. In that history of the evolution of the universe, the history of our earth and then, within it, our own history seems to be very small, even minute. And yet, if we remember that man has existed for three million years at least, we should not forget that Abraham did not appear until 1,800 years before Christ, who is the one whom we call Lord and not only the centre of our history but even the reason for it and what God had in view in his guidance of that history (see 'election' above, p. 94).

The world, then, and its history are involved in a process of liberation. This is because of Christ and because of us men and women. Because of Christ since his incarnation draws the world to him[7] and his redemption is cosmic. Paul speaks again and again — and not only in the captivity epistles — about this aspect of the mystery of Christ.[8] The Church Fathers believed that Christ's crucifixion pointed to it and praised the cross as the centre of everything. They saw it as a cosmic tree uniting heaven and earth.[9] But it is also because of us, since the universe is one and man is the end of it. The world is raised in him to the dignity of a person and he is himself a 'microcosm'. In this way, the world's destiny is tied to man's.

This can be justified rationally.[10] It is also implied in very many statements in Scripture — in Gen 3:17-18; Is 24:5-6; Jer 23:10, to name only a few. In Is 65:15-17 and in the book of Revelation, there is a close link between the 'new name' given to believers (Rev 2:17; 3:12), the 'new song' that they sing (5:9-10) and the 'new heaven and new earth' and 'all things new' (21:1, 5). Elsewhere, I have quoted from the remarkable address made by Mgr Ignatius Hazim, the Orthodox Metropolitan of Latakia, at the opening of the Fourth Assembly of the World Council of Churches at Uppsala in August 1968. The Metropolitan commented on the text 'Behold, I make all things new', describing the Holy Spirit as the agent of that process of renewal.[11]

Here as everywhere else, then, the rule is 'already, but not yet'. This means that we and our world are subject to a rule of waiting in hope and expectation — as Paul says so powerfully: *apokaradokia tēs ktiseōs* — *expectatio creaturae* — the 'eager longing' of creation (Rom 8:19). Creation is in fact at present 'subject to futility', in other words, to a condition of searching which is unending and cannot end or, as A. M. Dubarle has said, it is 'prevented from attaining that towards which it is tending'.[12]

Our history is impelled forward by an immense and impressive effort. I have tried elsewhere to show[13] that human history tends to overcome, on the one hand, the oppositions from which we suffer and to replace them by harmony, peace and communion and, on the other, the power of evil over good, injustice over justice, ignorance over knowledge and death and sickness over life and health. It is in this way that those characteristics of the kingdom of God that directly concern his creatures are revealed. We are not able to obtain for ourselves the fullness of reality and truth, but our effort has a positive direction and meaning. In this context, Paul speaks of 'groaning'.

Why do little children cry? They have, after all, no other way of expressing themselves. Their crying means: 'I need something. I am hungry. I don't feel well. I don't want to be alone. I want to be with others . . .'. They are, in other words, expressing the great forms of human misery. There is an obvious parallel between what we say and the Marxist analysis or programme, and this only emphasizes the entirely secular transposition in that programme of Christian eschatology.[14] A similar transposition of Christian theology can be seen in the philosophy of Hegel. I fully accept his idea that human history is a history of the acquisition of freedom or liberation. This is confirmed by Scripture.

Paul also makes use of the image of a woman in labour. This is a very common image in Scripture, where it is usually employed to describe pain during a time of trial.[15] It is nonetheless a positive experience — we suffer, but we give birth to something. Groaning and pain foreshadow a birth (see, for example, Is 66:7-14; Jn 16:21; Rev 12:2). Is it going beyond the meaning of the Pauline text to say that this world and, in it, believers who possess the first-fruits of the Spirit are contributing in their pain and tears to a birth? The Spirit is in labour with them and in them — in believers, certainly, but also in the world and in history.

The words of Wisdom are relevant here: 'Thy immortal breath is in all things' (12:1). The Old Testament authors saw the breath of God as filling not only man, but every living being (see, for example, Ps 104:28-30; Job 34:14-15). That 'breath' cannot as such be identified with the Holy Spirit, who had not at that time been fully revealed. We are more enlightened now and have, for instance, the documents of the Church Fathers, the theologians, the mystics and the documents of Vatican II. In all these writings, the active presence of the Holy Spirit is recognized in the world and in its constant seeking.[16]

This does not mean, of course, that everything in that history comes from the Holy Spirit. Evil also has a share and man is always *incurvatus in se*. He is permanently tempted to be 'turned in on himself' — to seek only himself and satisfy himself while ignoring and even despising God.[17] The Holy Spirit is the advocate of Jesus Christ and his disciples and as such he is the one who 'convinces the world of sin' (Jn 16:8-9). He gives impetus to the struggle against the 'flesh'.

Let us confine ourselves, however, simply to the positive aspect. The activity of the Spirit in the history of man and his world has as its aim the constitution of a body of the sons of God in Jesus Christ, a temple of 'worship in spirit and truth'. This can only be at the same time the Body of Christ (see Jn 2:21). Men — both the Jews and Solomon and those who built our great cathedrals — have always wanted to give symbolic expression to the whole material and human cosmos in their temples.[18]

In the great martyrology of Christmas, we sing: 'God, who wanted to consecrate the world by his merciful coming . . .'. This expresses the link between a latent cosmism, as I have called it, and the positive history of salvation, which Jesus embraces and of which he is also the centre. This is, of course, the Church, but it is also those unknown dimensions of the mystical body of the sons of God who are incorporated into the Son.[19] The Body of Christ, consisting of those who are in communion with Christ, has a visible form that can be named — the Church — but, as Paul Evdokimov has correctly pointed out, it may be possible to say where the Church is, but not possible to say where it is not.

We simply do not know the frontiers of the Spirit's activity in this world, nor the ways in which he acts. We can only be sure that they are related to Christ, whose spiritual body is formed with men by the Spirit. An attempt was made in the Decree on the Church's Missionary Activity, *Ad Gentes divinitus*, to give clear reasons for that activity. The conciliar document finally concluded that: 'The plan of the Creator, who formed man in his own image and likeness, will be realized at last when all who share one human nature, regenerated in Christ through the Holy Spirit and beholding together the glory of God, will be able to say "Our Father" ' (7, 3). A note containing several quotations from the Church Fathers is added to this statement, including one part of a text from Hippolytus, which I give in full:

> He rejects none of his servants, . . . wishing all and desiring to save all, wishing all the excellence of God's children and calling all the saints in one perfect man. For there is only one Child (Servant) of God. It is through him that we also obtain regeneration (new birth) through the Holy Spirit, aspiring to form together one single heavenly and perfect man.[20]

And it is true that only one man really says: 'Our Father'. As for us, the Church, we form in this great world what Paul called the 'first-fruits' and

what sociologists call a 'cognitive minority'. We know and we call Christ and
the Spirit by name. We have the inspired Word, the sacraments and the
instituted ministries. The Spirit is also active beyond the visible frontiers of
the Church and, for the world, the Church is the sacrament of Christ and his
Spirit. We include this great world in our prayer, interceding for it. We also
include it in our doxology, giving praise and glory for it to the Father through
Christ in the Spirit. For the Spirit is the one who in secret gathers up and
binds together everyone who is trying to stammer the words 'Our Father' in
this world. This is the meaning that I personally give every day to the
doxology that concludes the anaphora and introduces the 'Our Father' in the
Eucharist. The Spirit is, after all, the one through whom we cry or who cries
for us: 'Abba! Father!' (Rom 8:15; Gal 4:6).

Notes

1   J. Moltmann, 'Heiliger Geist in der Geschichte', *Orien.* 47 (15 June 1983),
    128-130.
2   *Duplex est creatio: quaedam in esse naturae, quaedam in esse gratiae... De prima*
    dicit Ecclesiasticus (17:1): 'Deus creavit de terra hominem', scilicet ut esset; de secunda
    creatione, Psalmus (103:30): 'Emittes Spiritum tuum et creabuntur', scilicet in esse
    gratiae, ut essent boni, 'Creation is twofold, one is the creation of nature and the
    other is that of grace... Of the first, Sirach says (17:1): "God created man out of
    earth", clearly so that he might be. Of the second creation, the Psalmist says
    (104:30): "When thou sendest forth thy Spirit, they are created". This is clearly
    the creation of grace, so that they may be good': Bonaventure, *De S. Patre nostro*
    Francisco sermo 3 (Quaracchi ed., IX, p. 583). This text is quoted by H. de Lubac.
3   See Regin Prenter, *Spiritus Creator. Studien zu Luthers Theologie (FGLP* 10. Ser.,
    6; Munich, 1954), pp. 187ff. It is the Spirit who makes the letter of Scripture into
    a Word of God, which is for that reason the living presence of Christ in us. He is
    the Word. See pp. 111, 115.
4   Ignatius, *Rom.* VII, 2. For the filial life, see *I Believe in the Holy Spirit* (London
    and New York, 1983), II, pp. 104-106 and 217-218.
5   This was also Luther's position. See Regin Prenter, *op. cit.,* pp. 194ff., 238ff. See
    also F. Schumann, *Vom Geheimnis der Schöpfung. Creator Spiritus et Imago Dei*
    (Gütersloh, 1937).
6   Let me quote here, despite its length, a passage from Walter Kasper, *Jesus the*
    Christ (London and New York, 1976), pp. 267-268:
       The Christian conviction is that there is only one instance in history where the
       Spirit found acceptance in a unique way, totally, undistorted and untarnished
       — in Jesus Christ. In the power of the Spirit he was wholly a mould and
       receptacle for God's self-communication through the Logos. He is this in an
       utterly unique way, so that he is God's love, the meaning of all reality, in
       person. The universal historical activity of the Spirit therefore reached its goal
       in him in a way that is ultimate. Light falls from Jesus Christ on the rest of

history; Jesus Christ is for the Christian the measure and criterion for the discernment of spirits. Only through him and in him is it possible to share in the complete fullness of the Spirit. Conversely, it is also true that the plenitude and full riches of Christ in Christianity will only find realization when the Spirit-inspired riches of the nations have found entry into the Church and have been 'sublated' in the Church. The mission and conversion to Christianity are always both crisis and fulfilment.

A Christology in a pneumatological perspective is therefore what best enables us to combine both the uniqueness and the universality of Jesus Christ. It can show how the Spirit who is operative in Christ in his fullness, is at work in varying degrees everywhere in the history of mankind.

7   See Cajetan, *Comm. in IIIa* q. 1, a. 1, no. VII: *Incarnatio est elevatio totius universi ad divinam personan* ('The incarnation is the raising of the whole universe to the level of the divine person'). See also C. Journet, *L'Eglise du Verbe incarné* II (Paris, 1951 [no Eng. trans of this vol.]), p. 270.

8   See 1 Cor 8:6; Rom 11:36; Col 1:16-20; Eph 1:10; 4:10. See also H. Biedermann, *Die Erlösung der Schöpfung beim Apostel Paulus* (Würzburg, 1940); A. D. Galloway, *The Cosmic Christ* (London, 1951); F. Mussner, *Christus, der All und die Kirche* (Trier, 1955). And, of course, Teilhard de Chardin.

9   See the last text, attributed to Hippolytus ['pseudo-Chrysostom'], in the remarkable anthology at the end of H. de Lubac, *Catholicism* (London, 1950), where other references will also be found.

10 See, for example, A. Franck-Duquesne, *Cosmos et gloire. Dans quelle mesure l'univers physique a-t-il part à la chute, à la Rédemption et à la gloire finale?* (Paris, 1947).

11 See *I Believe in the Holy Spirit, op. cit.* (note 4), II, pp. 33-34. The complete text will be found in *Irén.* 42 (1968), 344-359 and in *FV* (November-December 1968), 8-23.

12 A. M. Dubarle, 'Le gémissement des créatures dans l'ordre divin du cosmos (Rom 8,19-22)', *RSPhTh* 38 (1954), 445-465, especially 456.

13 See my *Lay People in the Church* (London and New York, 1957), pp. 59-118.

14 See A. Jäger, *Reich ohne Gott. Zur Eschatologie Ernst Blochs* (Zürich, 1969); J. Moltmann, *Theology of Hope* (London and New York, 1967), esp. pp. 304ff. I, on the other hand, wrote (*Lay People in the Church*, p. 93): 'the Kingdom will be an order wherein each thing will be in possession of its integrity and all will be at peace with one another because they are at peace with God, and this through perfect submissiveness to God, the power of Jesus Christ and the full influence of the Spirit'.

15 See Is 13:8; 21:3; 26:16-18; Jer 4:31; 6:24; 13:21; 22:23; 30:6; 48:41; 49:24; 50:43; Hos 13:13; Mic 4:9-10; Ps 48:6; Sir 48:19; Mt 24:8; 1 Thess 5:3.

16 See the conclusion of my *I Believe in the Holy Spirit, op. cit.*, III, pp. 271-272. For Vatican II, see the Pastoral Constitution on the Church in the Modern World, *Gaudium et Spes* 41, 1: the Holy Spirit is active in the religious needs felt by men; 26, 4 and 38, 1: every moment towards justice and every 'putting aside of love of self' is attributed to the activity of the Spirit.

17 Aspects of rejection and sin and the constant need for conversion and purification are frequently mentioned in the documents of Vatican II. See, for example, *Ad Gentes divinitus* 8 and even *Gaudium et Spes*. See also J. de Bacciochi, 'Le Saint-Esprit et la signification du monde', *VC* XXI, 81 (1967), 1-25.

18 For Solomon's Temple, see my *The Mystery of the Temple* (London and New York, 1962), pp. 94-100. For this phenomenon in general, see Mircéa Eliade, 'Prestiges du Mythe cosmogonique', *Diogène* 23 (1958), 3-17; and especially C. von Korvin-Krasinski, 'Die Schöpfung als "Tempel" und "Reich" des Gottmenschen Christus', H. Emonds (ed.), *Enkainia. Gesammelte Arbeiten zum 800 jährigen Weihegedächtnis der Abteikirche Maria Laach* (Düsseldorf, 1956), pp. 206-229, which containes very full documentation and cites the examples of Borobudur in Java and the Big House of the Delaware Indians; the reference to Christ is explicitated on pp. 214ff.

19 See the section 'The Dimensions of the Spiritual Temple' in *The Mystery of the Temple, op. cit.*, pp. 188-203, especially pp. 197ff.

20 Hippolytus, *De Antichristo* 3 (*PG* 10, 732; *GCS* [Berlin] 1, 2, 6).

By way of a conclusion

In order to speak clearly about the Word and the Breath I have, I know, run a serious risk of discussing them separately, whereas they work conjointly. They work conjointly because they do the same work — that of Christ. It is possible to say either, with Nikos Nissiotis, that Christ is the precursor of the Holy Spirit, since, as Athanasius said, 'the Word assumed flesh so that we might receive the Holy Spirit', or that the Holy Spirit is the 'vicar of Christ'.[1] He is, in other words, the one who has made Christ's work present here and now since the latter's physical 'departure' from us. Both views are correct, but they have to be distinguished.

The Church comes from Christ's incarnation–baptism–passion and from a Pentecost made constantly present. The two great activities of his ministry, the word and the sacraments, come from the Word and are life only through an epiclesis in which the coming of the Spirit is implored. The Word brings definition, but the truth can only be a saving truth for us through the action of the 'Spirit of truth'. We only see if we have first heard and we only really hear if we do the truth.[2] Revelation occurred once only. Its centre and its peak is Jesus Christ. In that sense, it is closed. But it is spread out in time and space by the action of the Holy Spirit. I could perhaps — and possibly should — have developed in this book a theology of Tradition and have included a chapter on the *magisterium* and its place in the communion of faith of the whole People of God. I have dealt briefly with this elsewhere. But it seemed enough to me to situate the status of the entire life of the Church as both Christological and pneumatological. I have also tried to show that the institution is based on charisms and, following the teaching of St Paul, that the operation of those charisms produces the institution.[3]

Before and in view of this, Jesus is only Christ and Lord through the Holy Spirit. (This is 'pneumatological Christology'.) But the Holy Spirit is only given and, in this sense, there is only a Spirit at all (see Jn 7:39) if Jesus is Christ and Lord. At a more radical level, in the eternal life of God, the Spirit is the Spirit of the Word. The latter is, in the words of Thomas Aquinas, not any Word, but the Word defined as the co-principle of Love: *Verbum non qualecumque, sed spirans amorem*.[4]

It is, then, not possible to develop a pneumatology spearately from the Word. Möhler made the attempt and drew the conclusions therefrom between writing *Die Einheit* and *Symbolik* (1825-32). The Holy Spirit is active in the cosmos and is the *Spiritus Creator* only because he is one with the Word and with 'God'.[5] We are therefore led to develop a theology of the Tri-unity that God is. He is, as it were, three times himself, in himself and with himself — in his Principle or his nature, in his Knowledge of himself and in his Love.[6] The Fathers and the theologians often cited Eph 4:6 with this meaning in mind: 'one God . . . who is above all and through all and in all'. In the same way, there are constant statements in the writings of the Fathers and in the liturgy that God achieves everything through his Word in the Holy Spirit. That is, going from us to him, the formula of our doxologies. I could perhaps — and possibly should — have developed further some of the aspects that have been only touched on in this book. I would regard the following as among the more important:

There is the question of the complementarity or the unity without confusion of the priesthood and that of the ministry with the whole body of believers, bearing in mind the priestly character of the latter as the People of God, the Body of Christ or the Temple of the Holy Spirit. It is even possible to speak here of a unity between the *magisterium* of the pastors and the sense of faith that is present in the whole body of believers, or of a unity between the 'apostolic succession' of the Church's ministers and the apostolicity of the whole body.

There is also the question of the Church's mission and the related question of evangelization. The second word is tending now to be used rather than the first, without disqualifying it. This is quite significant, since it provides us with a real link that unites the Word and the Breath. In the Apostolic Exhortation *Evangelii nuntiandi* 26,[7] Paul VI wrote: 'Evangelization is first and foremost bearing witness in a simple and direct way to God as revealed by Christ in the Holy Spirit'. In paragraph 75 of the same document, which is very long and full of biblical references, the part played by the Spirit in the work of evangelization is outlined in detail, beginning with Jesus and noting the activity of the Spirit in the struggle against demons and idols. There is also, of course, the Decree on the Church's Missionary Activity, *Ad Gentes divinitus*, to which I have referred several times in this book. Paragraph 4 is particularly striking in this context and I would cite its concluding sentence: 'Sometimes the Holy Spirit visibly anticipates the Apostles' action'. This statement is provided with a footnote referring to Acts 10:44-47; 11:15; 15:8. I have already cited the words of St Irenaeus: 'The column and support of the Church is the Gospel and the Spirit of life'.[8]

I have often drawn attention to the eschatological intention of the gift of the Spirit. In that sense, it can be seen as the ultimate Promise and the fulfilment and the consummation of God's work. The formula in the Creed that expresses it includes the 'resurrection of the dead and the life of the world to come'. I have dealt, albeit briefly, with this eschatological dimension of pneumatology in the final chapter of this book on the cosmic role of the Spirit, stressing such aspects as expectation, hope and the suffering endured in giving birth.

The eschatological element could be developed into a very positive vision of work — one that has been called Trinitarian.[9] Following the pattern of the Creed, work seen as creation refers to the Father; seen in its redemptive value, it refers to the Son; and as fulfilment tending towards eschatology, it can be interpreted as a reference to the Holy Spirit. This view therefore points emphatically to the tendency towards the kingdom of God which secretly inspires the history of mankind.

A subject that is so close to my heart that my readers would undoubtedly be astonished if it had apparently been forgotten, is ecumenism. This is clearly Christological. On the basis of the baptism which incorporates us into Christ and the Word which is our Christian norm, its aim is to carry out the will and the prayer of Christ, which is that his disciples should be united. It is also fundamentally pneumatological. The excellent Decree on Ecumenism, *Unitatis Redintegratio*, promulgated by Vatican II, which contains twenty-one references to the Holy Spirit, begins by recognizing that the ecumenical movement is 'fostered by the grace of the Holy Spirit' and concludes by saying that Christians should 'go forward ... without prejudging the future inspiration of the Holy Spirit'.

How and to what degree does the grace of Pentecost play a part in the disunited churches? Under what conditions can a theology of the variety of charisms be applied to them? How should the dialectical tension between 'diversity' and 'communion' be conceived and put into effect? It calls for an immense effort on the part of Jesus' disciples. It calls above all for effort on the part of the Catholic Church, which looks back at Jesus and at its own origin and forward to the fulfilment to which the Breath is urging and leading it.

Veni, Creator Spiritus!

Notes

1   See not only Tertullian, a Latin Father: *De Praescr.* XXVIII; but also Origen, who was a Greek: *Hom. in Luc.* XXII, 1 (*SC* 87, p. 301).

2 This is not simply a question of pragmatism or the fact that we only really 'listen' when we put it into practice. It is the biblical affirmation of the integrating character of faith, our coming to faith and the growth of that faith. See I. de la Potterie, *La vérité dans S. Jean* (Rome, 1977), II, chapter 6.

3 See C. Perrot, 'Charisme et institution chez S. Paul', *RSR* 71 (1983), 81-92.

4 Thomas Aquinas, *In I Sent.* d. 15, q. 4, a. 1, ad 3; *De Pot.* q. 10, a. 4; *ST* Ia, q. 43, a. 5, ad 2; *Comm. in ev. Ioan.* c. 6, lect. 5 (Marietti ed., no. 946).

5 This is clearly seen in Protestant theologians, who like to speak of the Spirit as creator. For Luther, see R. Prenter, *Spiritus Creator. Studien zu Luthers Theologie* (Munich, 1954). See also T. F. Torrance, 'Spiritus Creator. A Consideration of the Teaching of St Athanasius and St Basil', *Theology in Reconstruction* (London, 1965), pp. 209-228; G. Widmer, 'Saint-Esprit et théologie trinitaire', F. J. Leenhardt *et al.*, *Le Saint-Esprit* (Geneva, 1963), pp. 107-128.

6 Thomas Aquinas expressed the mystery in this way: see *Comp.* I, c. 50.

7 Published 8 December 1975 (*DC* 73, no. 1689, pp. 1-22).

8 Irenaeus, *Adv. Haer.* III, 11, 8 (*PG* 7, 885; *SC* 211, p. 116; ed. W. W. Harvey, II, p. 46).

9 G. Piana, 'Human Work: Blessing and/or Curse?', *Concilium* 160 (1982), 66-71, especially 69-70.

Principal works by Yves Congar

Chrétiens désunis (1937): *Divided Christendom* (1939)
Esquissses du Mystère de l'Eglise (1941; 2nd ed. 1953): in *The Mystery of the Church* (1960)
Vraie et fausse réforme dans l'Eglise (1950)
Le Christ, Marie et l'Eglise (1952): *Christ, Our Lady and the Church* (1957)
Jalons pour une théologie du laïcat (1953): *Lay People in the Church* (1957)
Le Mystère du Temple (*Lectio divina* series; 1958): *The Mystery of the Temple* (1962)
Vaste monde, ma paroisse (1959): *The Wide World my Parish* (1961)
La Tradition et les traditions (2 vols., 1960, 1963): *Tradition and Traditions* (1966)
Les Voies du Dieu vivant (1962): *The Revelation of God* (1968) and *Faith and Spiritual Life* (1969)
La Foi et la Théologie (*Le mystère chrétien*, 1; 1962)
Sacerdoce et laïcat (1963): *Priest and Layman* (1967)/*A Gospel Priesthood* (1967) and *Christians Active in the World* (1968)
Sainte Eglise (1963)
La Tradition et la vie de l'Eglise (1963): *Tradition and the Life of the Church*/*The Meaning of Tradition* (1964)
Pour une Eglise servante et pauvre (1963): *Power and Poverty in the Church* (1964)
Chrétiens en dialogue (1964): *Dialogue between Christians* (1966)
Jésus Christ, notre Médiateur, notre Seigneur (1965): *Jesus Christ* (1966)
Situation et tâches présentes de la théologie (1967)
L'Ecclésiologie du haut Moyen Age (1968)
L'Eglise de S. Augustin à l'époque moderne (*Histoire des Dogmes* series; 1970)
L'Eglise une, sainte, catholique, apostolique (*Mysterium Salutis*, 15; 1970)
Ministères et communion ecclésiale (1971)
Un peuple messianique, Salut et libération (1975)
Eglise catholique et France moderne (1978)
Je crois en l'Esprit Saint (3 vols., 1979, 1980): *I Believe in the Holy Spirit* (3 vols., 1983)
Diversités et communion (1982): *Diversity and Communion* (1984)
La Parole et le Souffle (1984): *The Word and the Spirit* (1986)